Dogs: Funny Side Up!

Nola Lee Kelsey's Funniest Canine Chronicles
from Dogtown to Bangkok

Nola Lee Kelsey

DEV
DogsEyeViewMedia

ISBN: 978-0-9802323-2-5

Library of Congress Control Number: 2008904387

Edited by Valerie Stone of SIQ Consulting & Research (drstone@assesscompetency.com) and Jeanne Modesitt

Cover design by Nola Lee Kelsey

Printed in the United States of America

Contents

To Dad

without whom there would be no Dog's Eye View

and

to everyone who has ever given a shelter dog or cat
a loving, life-long home

You are all heroes!

"The great pleasure of a dog is that you may make a fool of yourself with him and not only will he not scold you, but he will make a fool of himself too."

Samuel Butler in note-books of

"Higgledy-Piggledy," 1912

Nola Lee Kelsey

Introduction

The lamb in line in front of me edged ever closer to the time clock. It had been another long day at Best Friends' Dogtown. The next thirty seconds would be interminable. Heat and exhaustion had taken its toll on my perception of time. A bra full of dog hair and desert sand did nothing for my disposition.

On the floor below the time clock sat a box containing complimentary employee copies of the latest issue of Best Friends Magazine. Just as it was his turn to log out, the lamb froze. He glanced down into the box and began to browse through a magazine - with his tongue.

Exasperated by this inconsiderate blockade, I sighed with audible disgust and reached past. The little lamb glanced up at me sheepishly. My workday ended as it had begun. With a few pushes of the time clock's buttons my precious introvert's sovereignty was regained.

A long walk across the parking lot brought freedom from the military-like regimen of working at Dogtown's Lodges. An eternity had passed since the peaceful bliss of cool morning walks with the Lodge area dogs. Feeding, sweeping, hauling water, poop scooping, scrubbing pools and the occasional chasing of a rattlesnake had all lost their usual thrill amid the sweltering, hundred plus degree temps of southern Utah's desert.

It was not until I arrived home, not until I power-washed away the layers of sand and dog hair that sweat had adhered to my body that my mind began to unwind. Wait a second! Something was amiss. Suddenly, it occurred to me. That little lamb could never have actually signed out on a time clock. What was I thinking? He was too short. He'd never reach the buttons.

Fact is, it was probably slightly odd to have hoof stock in line in the first place. Was he on staff? I heard we were looking for a new dog trainer. Must be in charge of shepherds and sheepdogs, I deduced. Yea, that must be it. My Mamma didn't raise no dummy. Harnessing up my own dogs for evening walks, the circle of my life continued.

The bizarre becomes commonplace when you work with animals. Best Friends Animal Society was no exception. A Blue and Gold Macaw would be dining alfresco, perched majestically upon the steering wheel of a rickety old golf cart, yet the staff would walk past without skipping a beat. When I spotted a toy poodle and another little critter walking on leash together through Dogtown's parking lot, my initial thought was, "That terrier has the worst shave-down I've ever seen. Is the groomer on vacation?"

When I realized I was actually watching a poodle and a tiny goat being exercised together, I felt stupid. Of course it was a baby goat. Aren't they all leash-trained? Whew! Everything was normal again. Perhaps

I spent too much of my youth in Sturgis, but a potbellied pig in a Harley shirt and skull cap did not even rate a second glance anymore. Ho hum.

Prior to Best Friends, I'd been rescuing animals in Northern Thailand. Unlike the sanctuary, hope for animals in Southeast Asia was fleeting. There was no money for such misguided indulgences as animal rescuing. To spay and neuter is uncommon in Buddhist society; suffering, mange and starvation are not.

Perhaps it was necessary for sanity, but in Thailand I continually managed to find something to laugh about. Good language barriers and catastrophic travel disasters are like nitrous oxide to me. Toss in monks, puppies and the bizarre scenarios rescuers unwittingly stumble into on a daily basis, and a satire writer is immersed in pure gold.

So, what had happened? Why had I stopped laughing when I worked here at Best Friends, a place of hope? Perhaps my funny-bone had been buried in one of the feral dog runs? But which one? There is no doubt that for someone like me, Best Friends should be a riotously fun place to work, despite the hardships and cruelty we often see.

Then it hit me! I knew what was missing. In Thailand, I wrote. Contorting life's strangeness into words, I wrote travel articles. I wrote promotional stories for rescues. I wrote to educate people about animals, always with humor (almost always). I wrote for hope, the hope of saving even one animal's life.

Pre-Asia, I'd written about the wildlife I worked with, the deaf dogs in my home, even my backyard farm. Bringing light to the funny side of intensely ordinary or totally bizarre moments is what I do. Without humor, ordinary is, well, um, it's ordinary. That will never do!

With the work load at the sanctuary and my own dogs at home, I'd forgotten myself. Too busy to write and too exhausted to think, I was becoming "normal." No. That also would never, ever do. So I began to write again and I have not stopped. Once I started thinking again, the fun returned to my life with animals.

People, especially those of us who work with difficult cases, often start taking dogs intensely seriously. Don't! For to forget the comedy and laughter animals bring into our lives is to forget one of the main reasons we love and protect them in the first place. Everything is simply happier with pets around.

You hold in your hands a hodgepodge collection of my favorite canine chronicles, educational musings, jokes, tirades and promotional charity stories from the past few years. Some were previously published; others are new to the world. I am not bipolar. Each one is just a reflection of my mood at the time. Okay, so maybe I am bipolar. Fortunately that is of no matter here.

I hope I have compiled something for everyone. Some stories are borderline sweet. Many contain my preferred wicked satire. Different strokes for different folks, like pugs and Pyrenees. I hope to make you laugh. I'll probably piss you off. But I truly believe that together we'll dig up a whole lot of missing funny bones, remembering to laugh at dogs, at ourselves and thus laugh at life, along the way.

In the United States of America there are
approximately 75 million pet dogs.

Nola Lee Kelsey

A PittieFull Scenario

2008 marked the end of the first dog year of this millennium. Time changes so many things. In this new era, there are those who now assert that "forty is the new twenty" and "pink is the new black." Obviously folks cultivating these superficial one-liners are forty-something women who refuse to dress their age. That is not my point.

Yes indeed, the times they are a-changing. I personally foresee a time when pit bulls will be considered the new lap dogs. After all, according to the CDC, American laps are getting bigger.

Widening waistlines are not my only justification for this pitiful prediction. I offer several scenarios as evidence. But before I can begin to make my first case you'll need to meet three of Best Friends Animal Sanctuary's resident pit bulls. Each lives in an area of the sanctuary's dog department (a.k.a. Dogtown) called The Lodges. Could that be why they're called the Lodge Goddess Three?

Pandora - According to Greek mythology, Pandora was the first mortal woman and had very little will power (much like myself).

Hera – Hera was named after the Greek Goddess of marriage and motherhood. (Wow! Talk about getting the short end of the goddess stick! Why not just call her the Goddess of Continual Compromise and Taxiing Teens to Soccer Practice?)

Ophelia - This name is most renowned for belonging to a fictional character from William Shakespeare's Hamlet. (Note: Ophelia went a tad crazy before the final curtain, despite having never worked in Dogtown.)

You may b̶
these dogs is
they called
no idea. J

In a
to tell
rescued
very young age
resemblance to the othe
whimsical, fantasia-style name
Dogtown's Lodges. And, to add more
three of their cage identification cards show u
of a black, dumpling-sized pit bull puppy with big,
doe eyes.

This once seemed a tad bit odd to me. After all, Best Friends has a Cage Card Photographer Extraordinaire on staff. (That is my way of cleverly covering up the fact that I can not remember her name). We'll call her CCPE gal.

So one day good ol' CCPE gal turned up at Lodge Headquarters. As always she asked, "Nola, do any of your dogs need new cage cards while I'm here?"

Nola Lee Kelsey

"Well, yes, CCPE gal,"
new cards."
Explaining th
baby pictures
make our be
overlooked
CCP
(show
ask

I responded. "We do need some

...t three of the adult pit bulls still had
...n their cards, I made every effort not to
...oved CCPE gal feel stupid for having
...d them for so long.

...E gal immediately rattled off their names
... off). "Is it Pandora, Hera and Ophelia?" she
...ed. "Ah, yea, it is," I babbled, feeling quite stupid
...yself. That is when CCPE gal made the following
ironic statement:

"I've tried, but I can't get decent card photos of the goddesses. They're too friendly. They keep running up to kiss me on my camera lens before I get the shot. Then they just flop over for a belly rubbin'. By the time they stand up they're covered in dirt."

Mind you, CCPE gal is a pro. That all these dogs are black, an amateur photographer's worst nightmare, was not an issue. The problem was that the mighty muse of American whiners – pit bulls – were too loving and goofy to capture on film. To me this is a major qualification for becoming a lovable lap dog. To this day, Best Friends still has baby pictures outside these three dog runs (not to be mistaken for Three Dog Night).

Schmoozing passing paparazzi is not the only reason I believe pitties will assume their rightful position on American's large-n-lazy laps. Let's face it, not all of us want a dog so ridiculously small you can wear it in a locket around your neck. Pit bulls run a nice range of medium/small to medium/large. To me that's a happy medium.

For some of us, visible canines are simply safer to live with than those currently popular kamikaze-prone, minute, little ankle biters, which can sneak around undetected inside your average falafel. Besides who wants a pet they may have to pop out of their boot tread on a daily basis? Not to mention that fashion accessory pets may become easily lost on a ginormous American lap, only to turn up days later quivering underneath the remote control.

Historical trivia also supports the advantages of larger dogs draped over one's body. I once heard that the band Three Dog Night (not to be mistaken for three dog runs) got their name from an Australian Aboriginal tradition.

It was said that the Aborigines gauged the temperature of cool nights by the number of dingos they needed to keep their bed warm. A one dingo night may have occurred in early fall. But, a three dingo night? That was the historical equivalent of kicking the electric blanket up to high and folding it around your body like a burrito wrapper. It's a very cool story, if not the least bit accurate.

No doubt possessing a three dog lap is an unhealthy goal from a Jenny Craig point of view. Still, there are worse ways to live. Take, for example, life in a world full of Breed Specific Legislation (BS Legislation), suppressed individual freedoms, the tearing out of hearts and mass euthanasia of family members based on Nazi-level paranoia.

On an unrelated note: let's wish a happy and hearty "hello" to Legislators in Ohio, many of whom are rumored to be in negotiations with Mike Vick to head up their state's animal control department.

Anyone who believes they are qualified to speak against a dog's right to live in a loving family home, based on genetic ancestors alone should be required to pass these challenges.

First, hold my innocent looking, itty-bitty poodle mix on your lap for 90 seconds while he decides whether or not your manicure gets gnawed off at the elbow. Once released from the ER, there must be no bitchy whining for Old Lady Dog Legislation (OLD Legislation) or Poodle Mix Specific Legislation (PMS Legislation). Next, take a decent cage card photo of each of the Lodge Goddess Three. Once you've wiped away the slobber from their kisses, compare the two experiences. Now choose a dog to spend one week with. I dare you! If that doesn't change your mind, get therapy!

It's true. As an Animal Handler, I rarely dress my age or even my gender. All careers have hazards. But if pits as lap dogs rightfully become the next great trend in our country, then that is one bandwagon I am happy to hoist my ever expanding American waistline upon. In fact, my next hot pink, 2XL, low-cut, T-shirt will read: "Save a Pitbull – Eat More Ice Cream!"

"Breed specific laws are not based in science.
[Laws] banning breeds will not make you safer,
and the illusion that they will do so is dangerous
to humans and unfair to dogs."

Dr. Karen Overall

Nola Lee Kelsey

Sunshine's Tale

No day is ordinary when you work with animals. Routines contort around emergencies and nature's whims decide the schedules. The story is no different at Care for Dogs in Chiangmai, Thailand. Even the most casual mornings can change lives. When staff member Karin Hawelka sits down at her morning email, she has no idea what she'll find hiding in her inbox.

One day among the usual business letters, reports and million dollar stock tips cleverly disguised as spam, a glint of gold shone through. Karin received an email from a man who said he'd seen an underweight golden retriever at Doi Suthep temple. Martin, the alert animal lover who reported the dog, also noted that the retriever appeared to have a leg injury. The computer could wait. Karin and Care for Dogs' team member Ally Taylor set off at once.

Atop Doi Suthep Mountain lies the Buddhist temple of Wat Phrathat Doi Suthep. Perched high above the city of Chiangmai, the 600 year old sanctuary can be seen glowing amid rays of sunlight from all over the bustling metropolis below. The breathtaking views on the drive up the mountain would have been reason enough to escape the city. Still, Karin and Ally had a mission.

Among the shining golden Buddhas, bustling sidewalk shops and camera-heavy tourists, saffron-draped monks strolled the temple grounds. Zigzagging among the monks, the Care for Dogs' team added to the spectacle. Blonde-haired, white-skinned, farang animal rescuers intrigue tourists and Thais alike, though for different reasons. It wasn't long before the gals discovered their hidden temple treasure.

As reported, a beautiful golden retriever was indeed on the grounds. Sadly, the rest of the report was also true. The once magnificent animal was flea-infested, vastly underweight and limping along the temple walkway with no real place to go. At rest, the retriever's back left leg swung loose as if it were shorter than the others. Despite being in obvious pain the dog proved happy to receive attention and was easily handled.

As the duo made inquiries about the gracious canine, his story began to unfold. According to some street vendors, the retriever's owner just dumped the dog out of his car several weeks earlier, leaving the injured animal to fend for himself. While in Northern Thailand even the poorest vendors often feed abandoned temple dogs, at Wat Doi Suthep not a single one of these merchants carried a degree in veterinary medicine. Go figure.

On the surface, the story seems even more tragic in that no one cared if the team took the dog away. Occasionally vendors get attached to the strays they feed. Even a monk, often the last hope for abandoned temple dogs, was surprised to notice the wounded animal when Karen and Ally made their inquiries. "Please, take him!" he implored. In the end, this was the best thing that could have happened to the animal.

As Ally grabbed up their golden-fleeced find, Karin commandeered the temple's cable-car. This spared their new charge the 309 stair steps that are one of Wat Doi Suthep's more notorious claims to fame. Another is cable car crashes.

Within minutes, the trio was winding down the twisted mountain road toward the city and veterinary help. Despite the astronomical speeds at which Ally frequently drives, the brilliant orange canine found his new name before the truck blew across the Chiangmai city line. Sunshine!

X-rays revealed that Sunshine's left hind leg was indeed shorter than his other legs. The leg contained a metal pin from a previous surgery on his once broken femur. The pin should have been removed long ago. Having now migrated, a painful point was sticking out far beyond the bone. It had been this way for some time. Calcium now enveloped the steel. All the vet could do was cut off the extended end. Still, what a miracle this was for Sunshine! He was freed from what must have been many months of suffering.

When the Care for Dogs team transferred Sunshine from the veterinary hospital to their sanctuary, his true personality began to shine through. There is nothing like the confidence projected by a mentally well-balanced golden retriever. Despite his long hard spell, Sunshine proved worthy of his breed.

Dominant, yet not overly aggressive, he quickly established himself as top-dog in his area of the Care for Dogs shelter. Even against the resident Rottweiler mix, Noy, Sunshine drew a firm line. A peaceful balance was achieved among the eclectic mix of dogs.

In no time he stole the hearts of the Care for Dogs crew. Not surprisingly within a matter of days a pair of new volunteers, Teresa and Nok, informed Karin of their decision to give Sunshine a forever-home.

Karin smiled as she went off to check her email yet again.

Follow up: Care for Dogs (CFD) is always looking for volunteers to lend a hand with rescuing, facility maintenance, socializing the dogs at their shelter and more. Whether you're a visiting veterinarian, veterinary technician or trainer looking for some hands on work in a casual atmosphere or just an animal lover fashioning your own version of a volunteer vacation, you will make a difference. If you're going to be in Chiangmai and want to have an experience outside the tourist realm for a day or a month or if you would just like to make a donation, please contact CFD through their website: http://www.CareforDogs.org

The Humane Society of the United States estimates that 6-8 million cats and dogs per year enter animal shelters. Unfortunately, only 10% of pet dogs and 3% of pet cats are adopted from animal shelters.

Nola Lee Kelsey

Household Cleaning Tips

We have a new puppy in our home, Koko. I don't know if there is some cute designer name for a Siberian Husky, Black Labrador cross. Nonetheless, I'm convinced that if I properly rearrange the letters in those two breeds, it will spell out "Tsunami Dog of Destruction."

Somewhere out there exist seven other good-hearted families who wandered into Cedar Animal Rescue and adopted the remaining puppies from this same litter. God be with you. By now your dog has chewed the 9, 1 and other 1 key off your phone pad. Send up a flare if you need help.

Meanwhile, in the interest of making lemonade out of a lemon-headed dog, I decided to harness Koko's destructive energy and create something wonderful from this experience. I can't imagine what it will be. Meantime here is a handy house cleaning routine I've developed for other puppy owners. Pin it to your highest ceiling for safe keeping.

House Cleaning for Puppy Owners

Step 1: Shampoo the rugs.

Step 2: Put the puppy outside.

Step 3: Shampoo the rugs.

Step 4: Toss now unmatched shoes in the trashcan.

Step 5: Nail the trashcan shut.

Step 6: Match up your remaining three socks by length not color.

Step 7: Restuff unstuffed stuffed animals.

Step 8: Separate eyes of stuffed animals from poop using a garden hose and centrifuge.

Step 9: Place duct tape over holes in your garden hose.

Step 10: Place electrical tape over holes in your centrifuge cord.

Step 11: Put the puppy outside.

Step 12: Discreetly cover bite marks on wooden chair legs by wrapping them in torn underwear.

Step 13: Fill holes in sofa cushions with that funky Great Stuff® expando spray stuff dads love so much.

Step 14: Call and have your limit raised on Home Repair Store credit card.

Step 15: Send for a HAZMAT team to unclog the vacuum and clean out your lint trap.

Step 16: Gently wipe nose prints off of inside windows with a pressure washer and a vat of acid rain.

Step 17: Wash throw rugs then secure them back to the floor with a nail gun, four gallons of tar and Excalibur.

Step 18: Remove remaining dog hair from your home by moving.

Step 19: Affix household cleaning list and flare gun to the highest ceiling in your new home.

Step 20: Put the puppy outside.

Step 21: Enjoy your lemonade!

According to a study by the Centers for Disease Control entitled, "Which Dogs Bite?", chained dogs are 2.8 times more likely to bite! The dogs most likely to bite are male, unneutered and live on chains.

Attention Legislators: Please notice that "chained" is not a specific breed, neither is unneutered or male. Ban chains, not breeds.

Nola Lee Kelsey

NEWS FLASH!

Baghdad - A new human subspecies crawled forth from a Marine Corp tent in Iraq this week. Not one, but two of these hideous specimens were spotted videotaping themselves tossing a puppy off a cliff only moments after they'd been seen picking each other's noses.

Scientists immediately collected DNA samples to determine whether or not these two advanced forms of primordial scum were in anyway genetically similar to a former Atlanta Falcons Quarterback unearthed last year in North America.

According to Evolutionary Geneticist Dr. Ota Slapemfreaks of Gingivitis State University, "It's rare to discover one new hominid subspecies that evolved without a spine, much less two, on two separate continents, especially in such a short time frame."

Dr. Slapemfreaks went on to add, "The DNA similarities are quite astonishing. In fact, we're rerunning the tests just to be sure, but it appears Michael Vick may actually be the lost love-child of these two murderous Marines." Oorah!

While teams of trawl-wielding archeologists race towards the war zone to seek out more specimens, many in American Government have bought themselves a small but desperately needed clue. Congresswoman Sterl Lize-Themall proposed that the nation's cities abandon their fanatical, floundering and failed Breed Specific Legislation (BS Legislation) attempts. "I now see that we must move on to a more logical approach, cleansing the mammalian gene pool of vicious DNA strains," Lize-Themall announced. She then proposed Hominid Specific Legislation. The four guiding principals of the new regulations are as follows:

1) **Removal from the Gene Pool** - Puppy murderers and dog fighters would be immediately castrated or sterilized using precisely the same amount of anesthetic they gave the dogs before abusing them. Any living children of these offenders would also be immediately "altered". This additional compromise would save face for BS Legislation supporters who are mindlessly intent on insisting that genetics determine everything instead of just admitting they made a mistake.

2) **No Cost to the Public** – Bills to recoup financial costs for the sterilization and incarceration of this spineless hominid subspecies will be sent to whatever pro ball team or armed forces branch they are employed by. If they are not a member of any such organization, I'll gleefully pay the bill!

3) **Reuse and Recycle** - The supply of extremely tiny little balls resulting from the castrations will be sent to HuMenue Foods, mixed with Chinese wheat gluten and ground

into prison cafeteria meat. Estrogen will be added to help ensure that abnormally high concentrations of stupidity and cowardice will not be passed through the food supply.

4) **Decreasing the Trade Deficit** - There will be a mandatory 40 year incarceration after castration. Then these ball-less, spineless creatures will be embedded in clear plastic and sold as displays to casinos in Beijing.

Congress is planning to review the proposed legislation on a trip to a Jamaican Golf Resort later this month.

Meanwhile, in Iraq the video tape of the Marines throwing the puppy off the cliff has been seized. It was discovered that these two vile creatures weren't as stupid as we all thought. Filming themselves committing a heinous act of cruelty had perks. The two had a plan. Brilliant!

The Two, The Proud, The Marines needed the video to use as porn. It seems immersing themselves in horrific acts of animal abuse is the only way either of these walking primordial mishaps can achieve an erection. "Obviously this is a genetic glitch found in less evolved species," stated Dr. Slapemfreaks.

Back in America, an anonymous source reports that the city of Denver, Colorado has offered both Marines a spot on the town council in the event that they are bitch-slapped as far out of the service as they deserve to be.

One of the Marines involved, Private Evil Grinninfuck, is reported to have responded to the offer by saying, "Denver? Isn't that there one of them fancy omelet things? I used to light chickens on fire down back a uncle Baba's barn. He's also my grampy."

Nola Lee Kelsey

One female dog and her offspring can produce 67,000 puppies in 6 years if they are not spayed or neutered!

Nola Lee Kelsey

The Diva of Dogtown!

For some gals fashion is the staple of who they are. Theresa the dog is no exception. Even in the heat of a southern Utah summer she found a way to maintain her stylish side, without being over dressed. Not bad for a scrappy gal from the streets.

As best we can tell, five-year-old Theresa was "rescued" (a.k.a. bought) from a homeless man. Her rescuers (a.k.a. hoarders) probably never recognized what a diva they were about to have on their paws. Either that or they just could not maintain the pricey up-market tastes of this fabulous fashionista. Could that be why they abandoned her? Apparently these would-be rocket scientists forgot that accessories make the wardrobe. Theresa was wearing a microchip that was traced right back to the folks who dumped her (a.k.a. stupid move).

Nonetheless, for Theresa, eventually being rescued by Best Friends was her big break. The sanctuary is amply supplied with her favorite wardrobe staple - - giant red rubber balls she carries everywhere. Much like a pacifier, Theresa only spits the ball out when she is content. Once she's given prolonged attention by a favorite Caregiver or visitor, poof, out launches the ball. Much like any style-driven woman, she only drops her glitz and glam around those with whom she is truly comfortable.

When Theresa visits the salon at Best Friends, her groomer/style consultant, Molly Cook, always tries to find a bandana which coordinates with the flaming red ball. Molly has impeccable taste. Instinctually she knows the right bandana for the right dog. Be it a fluorescent retro design for a pug mix or red and white polka dots for a pretty pittie gal, Molly has it on hand.

In a recent interview, I asked Theresa what she felt it was that made her such a slave to style. Obviously she had given this question a lot of thought.

"If I'm beautiful, I might find a forever family to love me much sooner. You wouldn't know it now, but to see me without my designer duds, I actually look like a 48 lb wedge of moldy Helvetia Cheese. Plus, my ears are quite massive. But, when I'm all dressed up I feel quite pretty. The ball accessory is an old Oscar de la Renta trick I learned browsing People Magazine. Oscar is a personal hero of mine. He's the one who discovered that if you place an orb the size of a small Central American country in your mouth no one even notices your ears."

It's true. When visiting Best Friends most people never notice Theresa's ears. Oscar knows his stuff! Theresa truly is the Belle of the Ball. In fact we're now enhancing this diva's 'designer duds.'

Two weeks ago a volunteer brought Theresa a chic new rubber ball, only this one was orange. Bling! Bling! The result was a fashion renaissance! Molly promptly produced a new bandana covered with a color coordinating, orange slice pattern to complete the look.

Theresa is already reveling in the versatility of her expanded wardrobe. Little does she know, a Best Friends' Caregiver has ordered her a white rubber ball for more formal occasions (never after Labor Day, of course). Endless possibilities exist for this fab feminine pooch.

We occasionally get search and rescue organizations at Best Friends who look for dogs possessing a strong "ball drive" to work with. Theresa often dreams Tommy Hilfiger will drop by with a similar request. Though for this funny glamour girl a forever home would be the ultimate accessory. Her Gucci suitcase is already packed with hope.

Follow up: As of September 08, Theresa, Best Friends' Belle of the Ball, was still waiting for a loving, one-dog family to cuddle and to play dress-up with. If you need more hugs with added 'bling' in your life, please contact:

dogadoptions@bestfriends.org

You can view photos and read more about Theresa on Best Friends' Lodge Dog Forum at:

http://network.bestfriends.org/lodgedogs.

Nola Lee Kelsey

Chocolate contains theobromine, a substance similar to caffeine. Even a small amount can make dogs violently ill or even kill them.

Nola Lee Kelsey

60 Long Seconds

Normally I am against any more laws. That said however, I do wonder if people should be required to have an operator's license before they open their mouths.

Last spring I was standing at a charity yard sale when I heard the man in front of me mumble to his acquaintance, "I didn't know we had a new Humane Society in town. I've wanted to get rid of that white shepherd of mine."

Instantly I plunged into what I can only describe as an Ally McBeal moment. An intense daydream took over. The vision of me smacking this man in the back of his thick head was all too real. I could even hear the echo from his hollow skull. That's when I noticed my arm starting to raise up.

My brain contorted around his words. "Educate him with kindness, Nola," a good angel whispered in my left ear. Obviously this angel had gotten lost on the turnpike, for she was not mine.

"He'll learn more efficiently on the floor with your knee embedded in his trachea," my devilish life-long advisor sneered from the right. Hum? Both were viable options. Either way, I needed to think my speech through carefully before proceeding to educate this festering inferno of irresponsibility.

Practice Speech One

Listen up you ignorant toad, when you got your dog it was a commitment for life. No doubt a dead earwig would be better off without a lazy prick like you for an owner; however, you still have an obligation to exhaust every means possible in finding your pet the best home on Earth. Run ads, hang flyers, interview families, introduce your dog to other animals in potential new homes . . .! Buy a clue, you freakin' sloth.

Perfect! Now all I had to do was handcuff him to the donation box so he'd listen. Later I could attach a copy of my speech to an application for the Diplomatic Corp.

Okay, maybe I needed to go over it one more time, just to iron out the rough edges.

Practice Speech Two

Just how stupid are you?

"Breathe, Nola! Breathe!" The dastardly good angel reminded me. I turned backward only to see Sam, my Great Pyrenees. He was manning a Hugging Booth for donations. As his drool ran down a small child's arm, I could see only sweetness in Sam's eyes. Ah. All good returned to the world. That face could take the edge off a samurai sword.

Practice Speech Three

Excuse me sir, I heard what you said about your dog. You know, Three Springs Humane Society is just starting out. They don't have a lot of money and they need to be there for animals that are in desperate circumstances. If you feel you can no longer give your pet a good home, perhaps you can take some time (like more than a nanite) to place him with a new family yourself. I'd be happy to offer you some suggestions on how to go about finding a loving, life-long home. Then you'll know your shepherd's in a good place.

Okay. Probably better. A soon as I stopped Clarissa Flockhart from projectile vomiting maple syrup, I'd lay it on him.

Admittedly, in my heart I believed that my words would leave his skull faster than Brittany Spears can escape a child custody hearing, but one of us had to be mature. I breathed deep and turned back around. That's when I noticed his companion talking back to the dog-dumping-dimwit. She was speaking to him in sign language. The man was deaf.

McBeal returneth. This time in my vision I was eliciting a self-inflicted brain embolism by attempting to spell out my entire speech one letter at a time, mustering up whatever sign language alphabet I could recall from Junior High School. What was the symbol for F? It wasn't pretty. Obviously I'd need to summarize my thoughts. That's when I noticed my middle finger starting to raise up.

Did you know Nepal's capital city of Katmandu is on schedule to be a "stray-dog-free-zone" within 15 years, through a simple sterilization and vaccination program, not mass euthanasia?

Nola Lee Kelsey

When Dogs Choose You

Some lines were meant to be crossed, some dog breeds were not. Jake obviously knew this. He grinned menacingly as I left Best Friends' "Little Lebanon" compound on that frigid January eve.

Obviously, Jake was up to no good. I liked that about him. It was the first time the Best Friends staff had assigned me a dog to take on a sleepover evaluation. While I appreciated Jake's twisted sense of humor, he'd gone a bit too far.

Selected from the rows of German shepherds, lab mixes and a myriad of over-grown Hines 57s was my charge. Flipper. Jake told me to take Flipper. Two other Caregivers, Kerstin and Don, were normally eerily reserved. Yet both snickered and grinned from ear to ear at Jake's maniacal suggestion.

Flipper could only be described as a pint-sized, pasty-faced, West Highland Terrier, designer Poodle, cotton ball mix overstuffed with teeth and attitude.

Three months earlier the good folks at Best Friends Animal Society had evacuated nearly 300 cats and dogs from Beirut, Lebanon during the fall of 2006 conflict between Israel and Hezbollah. They were some of the most awesome refugees I'd ever seen, not like the dogs I worked with in Thailand.

Thailand's strays tend to be the purest of mutts. Most contain only a slightly recognizable vestige of some extremely fertile Welsh Corgi. I am convinced this one potent animal belonged to some 17th century Brit Expat who let it run amuck, humping everything in sight, as he ventured around Asia for the Dutch West India Trading Company.

The Lebanon Dogs were handsome, many of them purebreds. Most had the potential to be spectacular pets, despite having the tenacity to survive on the streets of a war zone. Unlike America's coddled canines, conflict and missiles plucked the weak and dim-witted from their gene pool long ago. I suppose it's not surprising then that Flipper was 80 lbs. of 'tenacity' in a 20 lb. body.

Fashion conscious, designer mutt breeders actually have a name for Flipper's probable cross – Westiepoo. I also had a name for this affront to nature – Absurd-a-Poo. There's no apology. I've always treasured big dogs!

Thailand's street dogs and America's deaf dogs; Dalmatians, Aussies and Bullies of more substantial size have always been my game. I'd gone so far as turning off Westminster when the Terrier and/or Toy Classes entered the ring, tossing popcorn at the TV screen and shouting, "Old lady dogs, yuck!" Big dogs are just in my blood.

At the time, I thought the Little Lebanon Caregivers had not understood that I had a background with, and preference for, cantankerous canines. Now I realize their actions were motivated by an instinct for self preservation. Even though they were some of the best Animal Keepers I would ever work with, not one wanted to crate Flipper at night if it could be avoided. Never mind being the poor sap who opened the violently convulsing crate in the morning. Cantankerous? Yes! Tragically, workman's comp can only cover so much.

Yes, indeed. The Caregivers of Little Lebanon thought they were oh so clever sending Flipper home with me. After the first night with him, I read them like a book. Not only were they practicing a good defense, they actually saw Flipper as a good match for me. In their eyes was some crazy-ass volunteer who strolled along quietly when she was forced to return from a walk with the jaws of Cleo, a shepherd mix, attached to her lower arm.

Better still, the gal had no dogs of her own. I'd just returned from Asia, where apparently I had a target painted on my forehead – shaped like a terrier. "There's no chance I'll adopt this dog," I warned.

Even Flipper ignored me. Once in my arms he'd call off any covert attacks he was plotting against neighboring dog runs and attach himself to me like a barnacle in a grey whale's belly button. True, Flipper did need someone with no other dogs. Why? Judging by his dog aggression, I'd say it was because Flip is 20 lbs of pure piss and vinegar on a good day.

I knew I was being subtly tag-teamed. My imagination jumped in on the game. On occasion I thought I heard Flipper whispering, "You're a zoologist. Overcoming my ravenous bite history will make me an interesting behavioral study."

Other times I had nightmares about the Caregivers' ulterior motives. "Get that yipping, dog aggressive, food aggressive, crate aggressive, barrier aggressive, cat aggressive, toilet paper aggressive gremlin out of our canyon. We're running low on band aids." A cold chill went up my spine with this description. Oh crap! Could Flipper be my soul mate?

Full days and long nights took over. The Lebanon Dogs were being prepped for a big adoption fair in Phoenix. I took dogs on outings, dogs on overnights, and dogs on drives. Observations of behavior, writing reports for their adoption files, and vacuuming my Jeep filled every free moment. But, something else began to happen. Every second night Flipper came home with me. First he was suggested then, to my dismay, he was requested. Had I gone mad?

Okay, so he was kind of cute. And around me he became fiendishly overflowing with exuberant kisses. As a rule he'd only try to pierce my skin once or twice a day. Even his obsessive unrolling of my toilet paper had a certain charm. Worst of all, his perfectly round brown eyes had an innocence about them. Wait! No! I would not let the maniacal little creature and his care giving conspirators lull me into their trap.

As I worked around Little Lebanon, Flipper would lay it on thick, shaking in his run and crying as I walked past with other dogs. He achieved an odd behavioral balance. Flipper could elicit pity from me one second and next launch an aggressive assault through the fence at whatever poor dog I was walking. If I dared to pick him up, the barnacle effect resumed. Justifying my cold-heartedness became a full time job.

"He's rage on a leash" I told Don one moment. Next I'd insist, "I'm too young for that Old Lady Dog." I'd also achieved an odd balance. "Which is it?" The caregivers drilled. "Is he too difficult for you to handle or too much of a lap dog?" Trapped! I'd been trapped.

Now all I could do was laugh nervously when the subject of adopting Flipper came up. Then, when no one was looking, I'd scamper off to the outhouse to hide. When Don nicknamed me something rhyming with Flippers Witch, I laughed even more. "Now where is that toilet paper?" Alas, had Flipper eaten it?

No doubt, I was still laughing as I filled out the adoption application. Perhaps I had gone mad. Denial is a hardy foe. Or perhaps it was time for an Old Lady Dog. It just happened to be my ?? Birthday.

The next day showed me the true generosity of the human spirit. I've never had so many caring people offer to fast track paperwork for me. All that morning trainers, managers, adoption counselors, and the like, would stop by Little Lebanon's campfire to chat. I'd glance over to see Don point towards Flipper, then somewhat aggressively point towards Dogtown's Adoption Headquarters.

Cars peeled out of the gravel parking lot like some dog-hair-infiltrated chase scene from the Dukes of Hazard. For hours, blinding dust choked the air along the three miles of road between Little Lebanon and Adoptions. Gosh, seeing so many helpful folks wanting to send Flipper permanently home with me was enough to make me teary eyed - - and drink in excess!

Eight months later it's all perfectly clear. Letting a dog choose us is one of the best parts about volunteering at Best Friends. I joined the staff not long after adopting Flipper. Since then, I've seen families looking to adopt puppies on Monday, leave at week's end proudly loading a senior dog from Old Friends into their station wagon. They couldn't smile any wider. Neither could the dog.

Workshop attendees have arrived by plane only to commandeer rental cars for cross country journeys when they were chosen by a dog with separation anxiety. Dobbie mixes charm poodle fans. Even with cats, it happens. Calico aficionados will have a tabby say, "No, I'm the one you want. You may take me home now." Somehow the chosen always know to listen - - even without Jake there to translate.

I believe people often have a predisposed idea of what they want and expect in a pet. When an adult shelter animal comes home, they are instantly hit with a different reality than what they envisioned. Puppies or kittens are sneakier. As they grow their unique personality slowly skews the person's perspective. Could the instant slap of an alternate reality be why some shelter adoptions fail?

What better way is there to select, or be selected by, a new family member than by volunteering? When potential families work around animals for a time they are naturally drawn to their perfect pet. A fuzzy soul mate. You don't have to travel to Best Friends.

Before adopting a pet from your local Animal Shelter, volunteer with the animals or lend them a hand at special events. In time you'll get a look inside the true hearts of potential pets. Prejudices of age, size, breed, or even initial temperament will be vanquished. You might just be surprised by what chooses you.

Nola Lee Kelsey

Thirty-nine percent of U.S. households own (or are guardians of) at least one dog.

Nola Lee Kelsey

Regarding Henry

Flipper entered my life with an ominous warning attached. "You understand you might not ever be able to have another dog around him," the adoption counselor warned. "Yea, I got it," was my half-hearted reply. Truth is, I was more likely to gleefully embrace the perks of global warming than live 15 plus years with only one dog in my life.

I mean, sure Flip was dog aggressive, food aggressive, crate aggressive, barrier aggressive, cat aggressive and toilet paper aggressive, but that could be worked with. Adoption counselors have to be cautious. I had to be optimistic.

With patience, training and several tubes of topical antibiotic, Flipper became a most fabulous companion. His food and crate aggression vanished, and of course, so did the crate. While he'll probably never allow a cat in my home (at least not a live one), hanging the toilet paper dispenser six feet up the wall did solve another of Flipper's issues. Things were looking up.

Still, something was missing. Each evening as I wrote, Flipper lay under my desk. Outside my window I could see neighborhood dogs playing in the field beside my home. They'd frolic, romp and run. Watching their joyful antics, I was saddened. Flipper had no playmates of his own. He always looked so bored. He seemed so lonely.

One day, as I entered Dogtown's Clinic, I heard the most hideous of noises. The sound can only be described as that of a heavily caffeinated, British ambulance siren withdrawing from crystal meth. It was coming from Dog Manager Michelle Besmond's office. With great hesitation, I peeked over her dog gate. Was Michelle indeed engulfed by paramedics? It was worse than I ever imagined. There, behind the gate, was Henry.

Henry's bark could peel the paint off of orbiting satellites. His physical appearance? Well let's just say Henry's got his own style goin' on. Think miniature Old English Sheepdog fornicates with a deoxygenated Ewok. Not only is he blue, but to add to his glory the poor bastard's eyes don't match, in color or size. Did you dare to guess? Tragically, Henry is an Aussie poo, an Australian shepherd, poodle cross.

I knew this poo would not do. Sure, the fact that he'd been abandoned in the desert broke my heart. He was spotted waiting loyally along the desolate gravel road for a family that had never returned. Still I felt no guilt when turning and walking rapidly away. Henry was so quirky looking I knew he'd find a home quickly.

Days later I was attending Best Friends' Dog Behavior and Handling Workshop. The first demo dog for intake evaluation procedures? Henry. He was still there. Worse still, he was steady and calm with a gentle confidence. In other words, Henry was the Anti-Flipper. Oh poo, I thought.

71

Somewhere in my mind I heard the sound of a fly-fishing reel. Henry was the lure. The hook was set.

In a state of foolish babble, I wondered aloud if Henry and Flipper might be able to get along. Like superman from a phone booth, Dog Trainer John Garcia leapt into the conversation. "We can try an introduction on Monday, Nola." Double poo.

Monday arrived quickly. As is always best for possibly problematic introductions, John and I brought each of the dogs to neutral territory to meet. We meandered along a sanctuary hiking trail, starting out a good twenty feet apart. The aggressor, Flipper, took the lead. He pulled backward, hopping along bipedally, while he snarled, barked and protested his way along the path. Blind rage on a leash! Every muscle in his tiny body tightened. In retrospect he looked more like a perturbed Tasmanian Devil-a-poo than a Westiepoo.

Henry simply trotted along obliviously waiting for Flipper to calm down and play with him. There was fun to be had. This boy was as clueless as he was blue.

As Flipper's rage lulled from exhaustion, the gap between the dogs was slowly narrowed. Once they walked calmly side by side for a time, John and I took them to the enclosed agility course to "play" together. At first we held the dogs on loose leashes while they sniffed (a.k.a. shook hands). So far, so good.

Next we dropped the leashes (a.k.a. emergency handles) to the ground. I wouldn't call what transpired a full-blown frolic, but it was a carnage-free first step. One more hike and "play" session later, I walked both boys into our home territory together. Flipper had a brother. Finally he had a friend to play with.

Each evening as I wrote, Flipper lay under my desk. Outside my window I could see Henry playing alone in the yard behind my home. He'd frolic, romp and run. Watching his joyful antics, I felt saddened. Henry had no playmates of his own. He seemed so alone.

And then there were three. Oh poo.

Nola Lee Kelsey

30% of dogs and only 2-5% of cats landing in shelters are reclaimed by their owners. Roughly four million per year are euthanized.

Nola Lee Kelsey

Great Pyrenees Grooming Tips

Introduction

Large breed dogs pose special grooming dilemmas. The Great Pyrenees and other Bernard family types have cornered the market on that special combination of girth and hair. Without a regimented grooming routine, the Pyrenees' flowing white locks will easily morph, soon resembling an electrocuted Komondor.

One obstacle to keeping large breeds in the peak of beauty is the difficulty in locating nail clippers, brushes and dental supplies suited to their substantial size. Substitution will have to be made. Still, with a little ingenuity, grooming will be a snap.

Body Brushing

Combing out the Great Pyrenees is a challenge. The high-strung nature of the breed makes them tend to wiggle around during grooming. In fact, these 'stealth' dogs are apt to sprint off if not restrained, sometimes moving up to three and a half feet in a single afternoon.

Your best bet for body brushing or raking their fur is to work on your pet while he is asleep. Avoid active times such as 6:00 to 6:03 a.m. and the 30 minutes after sunset Pyrenees devote solely to barking. Beware! This breed is known to sleep with its eyes open. When stalking them with grooming tools be cautious. Once you are within 65 feet of your dog, listen for a freight train. This verifies he is snoring.

Work efficiently. Once you begin grooming your Great Pyrenees, you may only have 13 hours before he rolls over, exposing oodles more work to be done. When grooming 140 lbs. of fur bonded together by drool and the occasional tree branch, time is your enemy. A weed eater is an efficient option for quickly working your way through the shrubs to the actual dog prior to brushing.

Dental Care

Dog owners often overlook the importance of good oral hygiene. They should also pay closer attention to their pet's teeth. Fortunately, in large breeds, their mouths offer plenty of room in which to work. Take advantage of this trait. You can create ample access to the teeth by simply pulling their massive floppy lips up from both sides of the face. Then, use three clothespins to secure the lips to one another across the bridge of the nose. You may also secure a single lip to the opposing ear in a similar manner.

Once the teeth are exposed, insert a Shop Vac® tube under your dog's tongue. This technique is identical to that of the spit-sucker used in your dental offices. A fifteen-gallon vac should suffice. Once the vacuum is fired up, your Great Pyrenees will start to be jolted awake. You will only have about two hours in which to completely remove the large pieces of sod stored along the gum line before your dog hits his full cognitive state. At this point he'll swallow the vacuum whole before falling back asleep.

Nail Clipping

Clipping your Pyrenees's claws should be a regular part of your grooming routine. Before beginning this procedure, head for the hardware store. Pick up a large metal rasp and bolt cutters. Once claws have been neatly trimmed, call in a construction crane to remove the clippings from your home. Don't forget the dewclaws.

Great Pyrenees have a multitude of extra toes just kinda "hangin' around" on their lower legs. Protruding out of them are massive curly toenails. Each is so large they make velociraptor claws look more like minute droplets of Chihuahua snot. On the plus side, if you weld three or four of these clippings together you will have a lovely new spiral staircase for your home.

Foot Care

As a final touch, clean your canine's feet. Shimmy up between the pads with a flashlight, some pliers and a bottle of WD 40®. Always take along a glow-in-the-dark chalk to mark your trail back out. Remove stones, dried bats, milk carton children and anything else not belonging up there. Once this task is done your grooming regime is complete.

Now wake your dog by simple whispering the word "cookie." By the time you get to "coo" every Pyrenees in a six county radius will be fully alert and standing in your kitchen.

Summary

With a little work and a few trips to Home Depot, your Great Pyrenees, Saint Bernard or Newfoundland will glow with beauty. When you combine all this glamour with the breed's high intelligence and electrifying charisma, your dog will soon be the envy of your neighborhood.

Nola Lee Kelsey

According to experts, two dogs, a Pomeranian and a Pekingese, survived the sinking of the Titanic. Also, according to experts, three dogs, a Newfoundland, a Pomeranian and a Pekingese, survived the sinking of the Titanic. There is also at least one report of four dogs surviving.

Nola Lee Kelsey

Rules Dogs Live By

Today we're going to talk about rules. Have you ever noticed that old people will suggest you hit your dog on the nose with a rolled up newspaper whenever it does something wrong? Yet, apparently, we're not suppose do the same to Dick Cheney whenever he opens his mouth. Talk about your mixed messages.

Unlike the Bush Master, dogs at least want to play by the rules. Don't they? Or perhaps the problem is that much like VP Dick, canines have their own perception of what the rules are. Consider these staple rules of dog society:

- If it can be stuffed, it can be unstuffed.

- Leashes should be pulled hardest when the ground is iciest.

- The neighbor's trash can is a weekly offering to you. Enjoy the experience to its fullest.

- Couches will always feel softer with mud on your paws.

- If Dad forgets to bring the poop bag to the park you must poop at all costs.

- If Dad brings one poop bag to the park, you must poop twice at all costs.

- If Dad brings two poop bags to the park you must instantaneously manifest diarrhea.

- If Dad is flirting with a pretty lady in the park, also instantly manifest diarrhea - - twice.

- When your owner drops the end of the leash, it's a surefire sign he wants to play chase with you in the street. Always accommodate these whims.

- If a cat moves away from you, chase it!

- If a cat moves towards you, run!

- To get every last drop of squeeze cheese out of a Kong, use the cat's tail.

- If it's set out to thaw it's for you!

- Nothing is more fun to lick than a clean camera lens.

- The dog barrier in Mom's car is a challenge you must always rise above.

- Paired socks must die!

- If a sock is already missing its match, leave it to suffer alone.

- Never have an accident on the easily cleaned tile floor if you can possibly make it to a freshly made bed.

- When Mom's date picks her up, bite first, hump second.

- Never dig in the gravel when you can dig in the grass.

- Never dig in the grass when you can dig in the garden.

- Never dig in the garden when you can dig under the fence.

- iPods®, they're not just for breakfast anymore.

Nola Lee Kelsey

A Massachusetts SPCA study concluded that those who attend dog fights are five times more likely to commit violent crimes against people.

Nola Lee Kelsey

Thailand's Temple of the Dogs

It was 5:45 p.m. and I was stalking an angel on temple grounds. As the rain started, I wondered if she would show herself at all. Chiangmai's rain patterns are directly correlated with the contents of my purse. The resulting meteorological phenomena means the rain could stop in a matter of seconds or pour down for days, depending on whether or not I'd brought my umbrella. I had not.

Squinting past the droplets, I glared up at the massive 700 year old Chedi, a Lanna-style stupa which draws in visitors from across Northern Thailand. Sure it's impressive, but what I want to know is: How can you have such a large building sitting there for over 700 years and never have gotten around to installing any doors? Surely it had rained here before.

Where to hide? No way would I take shelter in the two beautiful little buildings in front of me. Stunningly designed? Absolutely! But each houses a wax replica of an elderly monk sitting inside a clear acrylic box. Okay, I admit it. The first time I saw them I thought they were real. It took more time than I care to say for me to realize . . . Oh, never mind.

File those guys under 'way too real looking' to pass time with. What can I say? Lack of blinking disturbs me. Beside, if wax can achieve the lotus position, why can't I?

Escaping the deluge, my shelter took the form of an open-air gazebo housing three large gold-encrusted Buddhas. I would not be alone. One by one, temple residents trickled in. The first went straight to a mat he obviously kept laid out for these moments. Two more just sat down and licked themselves. By the time the skies opened up completely, three more temple dogs had meandered into our communal shelter.

Carrying dog cookies is just something I do. I could explain myself, but people either get it, or they never will. I tossed five treats out and turned to the sixth dog, Lek (Thai for little). She had vanished. Not possible. Why would she go back out in the torrential rain? Was there a dog door in the side of the ancient chedi?

Finally I surrendered her cookie to an antique looking Weimaraner. Predictably, that's when I spotted Lek. Out of the corner of my eye, I noticed her stretching out in the right hand of a sitting Buddha. She yawned, nestled perfectly into Buddha's arms and fell fast asleep. Very cool! After six years of visiting Wat Chedi Luang, the temple still brings a smile to my face. Must be why I keep coming back.

Actually, as the donation box says, "It all started about ten years ago." Ajarn Rosocon, a teacher at Chiangmai's Rajabaht University, decided to make helping the temple dogs of Wat Chedi Luang and the adjoining Wat Phan Tau her mission. 'Ajarn' is Thai for teacher. Her best lessons were taught at these massive temple complexes. Out of a potential hell, these magical Buddhist sites have been transformed into a sort of canine Nirvana.

Initially, students and friends helped Ajarn Rosocon care for the dogs. They fed, sterilized, vaccinated, treated for mange... whatever they could manage from the meager baht (pennies) they scraped together. The group was determined that the dogs of Chedi Luang and Phan Tau not suffer the life faced by the hundreds of thousands of sick and abandoned temple dogs across Thailand.

In 2005 Ajarn Rosocon unexpectedly passed away. Her friends, Ann Pierce, and a devoted student, Khun Soonthree, stepped in. Adopting Rosocon's cause as their own, they went forward, honoring a friend's memory by helping the helpless. As time passed, Khun Soonthree would become the new "Angel of Chedi Luang." Rosocon's dream and spirit became her own.

Wat Chedi Luang has become a refuge not just for dogs, but for all animal lovers. Travelers overwhelmed by the sight and plight of other stray dogs or simply in need of a quiet escape to rekindle hope frequently visit this 'feel good' temple. At 6 p.m. they watch for the angel. Over three years after Ajarn Rosocon's death,

Khun Soonthree still feeds and cares for the temple's dogs. Dinner is at six.

Word has it Soonthree never misses a day. She was there in the rainy season when her own home flooded, not once, but three times. She was there in the storm when Lek and I sought shelter among the Buddhas. Her bright yellow rain slicker and massive pot of steaming rice mix carried her through the tempest. If it's 6 o'clock in Chiangmai, she's there right now.

Most people visit Wat Chedi Luang to view the impressive ancient Chedi. In addition, its beautiful grounds are perfect for retreating to a quiet sanctuary in the heart of the city frenzy. Vendors offer food and cool drink. Trees and benches furnish hospitable shade. The adjoining Wat Phan Tau casts a luminous teak glow over the Buddha images it houses.

Adding to this peaceable cultural immersion, the aptly named "Monk Chat" area offers travelers a welcoming invitation to pull up a chair and, quite simply, chat with monks. The casual atmosphere where international visitors just 'hang' with Buddhist monks is a fabulous forum for asking questions and learning about one another's lives. In the background the voices of novice monks echo outward from the open classroom windows.

Of course, for a few of us the temples house one more special treasure – the dogs. Not all are social. Not all are loyal. Some are downright ornery. But to know the 'who's who' of Chedi Luang canines adds to the pleasure of a visit. True, most tourists barely notice them – except to do a quick sidestep away. Like many regulars, however, I've given them nicknames.

Take Ren and Stumpy, for example. Ren, a diminutive twig of a dog, is the duo's personality. Stumpy, with a malformed front leg contorted up underneath, provides a bit of size (a valuable asset in the world of temple dog politics) to the team. Side by side the pair can be found on a small patio overlooking the Chedi's north face.

Ren first works her magic, charming visitors with enthusiastic greetings. Then Stumpy shows his handicap, *Abracadabra!* Any traveler with half a heart makes a beeline for the ubiquitous '5 baht meat-on-a-stick' vendor. "No need to heat it, sir."

Then there is Lady. She works with a local artist by delicately charming customers to his postcard rack.

From there they get a close-up look at his lovely hand sketched works. I suspect Lady pulls in a commission.

Friendly Little Lek hovers at ordinary in the looks department. But every dog is beautiful when they sleep in Buddha's arms.

Not all is perfect. When I first saw Hiccup, I thought he had just been poisoned. Now I know the perpetual hiccup must be a medical problem. What exactly, I cannot say. While not overly social, Hiccup is stunningly photogenic.

At the front entrance of Chedi Luang are the three Golden Boys. At least I think they are boys. They rarely stand. This is the first place Khun Soonthree feeds each evening. Looking at the girth of the Golden Boys, it's a tad surprising there is any food left for the other temple dogs.

Across from them lives Lucy – the Teddy Bear dog. Had you seen her before her haircut, you would have expected to find a price tag and Steiff® snap in her ear.

No one knows exactly how many dogs live at Chedi Luang, 60+ perhaps. Other notable characters include Cookie Monster, whose cantankerous attitude and dull looks are well compensated for by the fact that he is the only one who actually likes the dull old dry dog cookies I bring on days I'm feeling broke. Apparently, others prefer Khun Soonthree's cooking to mine.

The latest I have noticed is named, "Oh Crap, Where Are My Ears?" Oh Crap..., or Ears for short, must be an abandoned pet. He is way too forlorn looking to be a tough guy from the streets. It's as though he desperately wants a master. However, he's willing to settle for jerky - or bigger ears.

Chubby, a pseudo red Chow, and Pigeon Chaser top off the list of charmers over at Wat Phan Tau. Pigeon Chaser will pass any domestic chicken strolling around the grounds, but heaven help the wild birds if he ever sprouts wings. The young monks at Phan Tau are especially loving toward their smaller population of temple dogs. It is truly a joy to watch them interact. Saffron robes and happy tails flourish side by side.

The influence Chedi Luang has on animal lovers is best summed up by Ann Pierce. A former volunteer with the dogs, Ann has returned to California, but wrote this in an email interview:

"I cannot begin to articulate the impact the dogs, Ajarn Rosocon, Khun Soonthree, Wat Chedi Luang and all the other people I met through my time in Chiang Mai has had on me. I'm a very different person because of my experiences. My dream is to one day move back to Chiang Mai and continue helping the animals, no matter how frustrating it is at times."

If you are visiting Chiangmai, you'll never regret taking the time to stroll around Wat Chedi Luang. You will regret not bringing your camera. Be sure to walk behind the main wat. Then circle the ancient stupa. Allow yourself a couple of hours, by not hiring a tuk tuk driver or guide to escort you. There is no need. You'll make one fabulous discovery after another. By the way, there are three donation boxes around the Chedi designated specifically for the dogs. Take the hint. You'd be amazed at how far Khun Soonthree can stretch these desperately needed funds.

Follow up: When I last spoke with Khun Soonthree, she had expressed a desire to expand her work into a few nearby temples. I believe strongly in her ability to help animals, one temple at a time. Of course she would need a dependable, long-term source of funding. Perhaps different families, groups or organizations could sponsor a different temple. Anyone? If you are in Chiangmai, you know where to find her at 6 p.m.

Other organizations that help pets in the Chiangmai area include Lanna Dog Rescue and Care for Dogs. Both have web sites and are always looking for volunteers or donations of funds, foods and materials.

In addition, Care for Dogs has a wonderful shelter offering adoptions of healthy rescued dogs and puppies to good homes. Remember, for each new pet that finds a forever family, space is made for another dog to be brought into their facility. For more information visit http://www.CareForDogs.org.

When you consider that 150 people a year die from falling coconuts, it means you are 60 times more likely to be killed by a palm tree than by a pit bull.

Palm Tree Specific Legislation:

Coming to a city near you?

The Dog Bite Diaries

Mom's Diary, Feb 23rd

Dear Diary,

Today I really messed up! I took all three dogs out for a walk together. I know better. What was I thinking? I totally set Flipper and Henry up for a problem (My Mistake #1).

It's been so cold. No other dogs have been in the park for days. Taking all three out at once has not been a problem. But, this morning the sun was out and I flew on auto-pilot. Standing on the river bank, I watched the ducks preen in the sunshine, blissfully unaware of what lurked along the path behind me (My Mistake #2).

Before I even heard Flipper hyperventilating, a nice Man who walks an adorable bichon mix (Red w/one white leg - - very funny) had approached to within 20 feet of my motley crew.

Days ago I talked to the man and played with his dog as they passed by our art gallery. I had not thought to tell him that if he ever saw me with my dogs, he should avoid us like we were a new strain of Ebola on a leash (My Mistake #3).

Today, Flipper went bipedal, sniffed the air and lunged for the bichon like a rabid version of Jack the Ripper. Henry attacked Flipper, because that is what Henry does. Flipper fought back. Next, Koko got scared, sat down and began a series of Husky howls.

I can't imagine what anyone witnessing this spectacle thought. Of course my dogs were leashed, harnessed, and attached to me, but the man and his sweet little red dog were last seen running north of Fargo, headed towards the Canadian Border.

As I pulled on the boys' leashes reeling them apart, I felt it happen. Flipper's harness began to slip over his head. It was loose (My Mistake #4). Flipper caught on instantly, tossed me a devilish look, and slammed his body into full reverse. It's funny. The harness slipped to the tip of his nose in under 1/100 of a second, yet time stood still as I weighed my options.

I could wire money to Montreal for Flipper's bus ticket home. Hope the bichon's owner would settle out of court. Or pray Flip would just take off around town wreaking havoc at every fenced yard until he encountered a loose rottweiler or Corvette. Odds were, he'd sniff the strange red dog once, growl, snap, then head into the forest at the park's northwest corner, returning later picking venison from his teeth, but it was still a gamble.

I thought about grabbing his collar. But if it slipped off (after he twisted and broke my fingers) he'd have no tags. That would leave him without identification, without his dog license and without that special extra tag saying, "Reward" on one side and "If you find this dog for the love of God keep him away from your other pets!" on the other side.

As my 1/100 of a second approached its meager end, I was left with only one option: grab a handful of

100% pure Flipper. Take hold of hair, skin, muscle, possibly a kidney . . . and hold on tight no matter what happened next. Of course, I knew exactly what would happen next. I grabbed Flip. And he "grabbed" back - repeatedly. Bite one, bite two, bite three. Once I lifted him off the ground he lost his leverage, and his thirst for blood. All went quiet as we rapidly crossed the bridge over the river, making a beeline for home. The leashed empty harness bounced along behind us.

While cleansing my perforated hand in the sink, I simultaneously kicked myself in my own ass (not bad coordination for a gal my age). Despite being raised in the Deny All Responsibility generation, I must admit it. I blew it – big time!

Flipper's Diary, Feb 23rd

Dear Diary,

I think my mommy has a bipolar bear disorder. Today she fed me cookies and rubbed my tummy before our morning walk. Then a few minutes later she scruffed me and tried to pull my pretty white hair out by the roots.

It all started when we were on a walk. A real live cowboy and his purdy little red dog walked up to say hi. I wanted to play chase, but Henry got jealous and ruined all my fun, so I beat him up. Stupid lil' sister Koko started crying – again!

Mom had been watching the plump and juicy looking ducks in the river one moment, then without warning her mind switched gears. She tore off my harness and grabbed my pasty little body with both hands. I thought she was having some sort of Dog Whisperer flashback, but that show wasn't on in the 80s. Was it? All I could do at the time was hold on tight to her in case she dropped me. Now, I am writing Dr. Phil for help – big time!

Mom's Diary, Feb 24th

Dear Diary,

Today one person after another noticed my hand and commented on how they would get rid of Flipper. My mind is incapable of working that way. It must be because folks these days refuse to admit making mistakes, let alone try to learn from them.

Not once did Flipper say, "Hey Ma, can you loosen my harness and walk a strange dog up to me?" or "What do ya say we all go over to the park and kick each other's ass?" He is not responsible for my absent-mindedness.

Human errors, such as not recognizing the importance in having pets spayed or neutered or by mindlessly buying puppy mill pets, already needlessly kills over four million animals a year in the United States. If artists and writers add to this by dumping our pets every time we happen to 'space out' that number would double in a month. I admit I lost my focus. I take responsibility for my mistake and I alone will bear the cost of the iodine - - lots of big time iodine!

At 5,000 years in the wild, the Australian Dingo is the oldest verifiable feral dog population. As of 2005 Australians themselves had 3,754,000 dogs that were still pets.

Nola Lee Kelsey

So Ya Wanna Start a Sanctuary

Many of us dream of starting our own animal sanctuaries. In my world you hear this fantasy so often you'd think shelters would be as common as soy at a vegan convention.

After two decades of working at, and volunteering for, every ilk of animal rescue, in addition to attending seminars on founding sanctuaries, and driving past many more, I fancy myself quite knowledgeable on the basics of sanctuary operations. This is precisely why I don't start one.

Still, others have braver souls. So if I'm correct, and I am quite certain I am not, these are the basics of founding an animal rescue.

To begin with you need to buy a large piece of land with a reliable water source. These are only affordable in locations where no life could actually live. Next you need a detailed plan for robbing Tiffany's in New York. If successful, you will be able to put a minimal down payment on the structures and fencing necessary for housing the animals.

While construction is going on, run to the office supply store. Pick up 32,000 ink pens and a bathtub full of White Out®. Now begin the paperwork involved in founding a nonprofit organization. Also fill out applications for housing multiple animals within your state, county, town, city, cruise ship and/or ark.

Note: Nonprofits should have at least five members on their Board of Directors. Consider your options. Look for people with skills in marketing, business, accounting and fundraising. Of course, this is a futile search among animal people. But occasionally you may find one of us who can balance our checkbooks.

Once you've exhausted yourself with this whimsical, self-deluding fantasy of perfection, grab five animal lovers. Heads up! Each will believe they are the Jane flippin' Goodall of the dog world. As a result they will be convinced they know what is best for every mammalian species to evolve since the Triassic period.

Ultimately your Board of Directors will be composed of one perpetual whiner, one overbearing bitch, two people incapable of compromise and the requisite vegan who takes every available opportunity to demand spinach as the facility's staple cat diet. FYI: If you stab this person with a letter opener, they will bleed green. At least that's what I've heard. I never actually . . . I mean . . . accidents happen!

Moving right along. File, in triplicate, extra applications for housing the most basic wildlife, such as road kill squirrels, with Game, Fish and Parks, the Department of the Interior, the State Wildlife Managers office and The A.U.A. – don't ask.

Next, file the paperwork for insurance, payroll taxes, business licenses, dog licenses, driver's licenses and the ever popular License to Hold Three or more Licenses.

By the way, prior to filing anything, shred whatever forms you may have used White Out on. That's not allowed. Get yourself a bathtub full of gin and start over.

Okay, now organize your marketing plan. Consider marketing your reason for drawing every breath, only a tad more important than oxygen. If not, animals will come in ninety nine times faster than they go out. Ironically, money will go out ninety nine times faster than it comes in. Win, win? No, no!

You'll need a marketing/promotions team who can maximize promotions at every opportunity. They must be capable of draining the smallest drop of publicity from every move your shelter makes. If they are doing their jobs right, Anderson Cooper and Barbara Walters should line up to mud wrestle for exclusive coverage of your annual dog jog. And of course, the loser should get the exclusive rights for coverage of the actual mud wrestling event.

Your PR team should even be able to see how saving a pug from a hangnail can be written up as a news release worthy of international distribution. Remember, this department is your rescue's life blood. Am I being too subtle?

While the mud wrestling pit fills, make sure you have a Keeper staff whose total qualifications are not limited to having watched a full season of the Dog Whisperer, especially if you have a cat rescue. You don't want behaviorally challenged shelter dogs being pushed to the ground by behaviorally challenged animal handlers even if they have calluses on their remote control fingers. Again, not win-win.

It is vital to limit the scope of species you choose to work with. No rescue can be all things to all animals. Your facility will fill to capacity inside two weeks if you are not selective. Of course, if you limit yourself to just dogs or cats, you'll be full in one week.

In fact, if you can limit the scope beyond just the species you work with, it would help. To keep from getting overwhelmed, I recommend something along the lines of, Noah's Rescue for Two-Legged, FELV Positive, Calicos with One Blue Eye; or for dogs try, Bruce's Sanctuary for Dog Breeds over One Hundred Pounds and Starting with 'Z'.

Of course, parrot rescues can draw a line by only accepting animals whose owners actually put in the minimal sixty year commitment owning an exotic parrot requires from the beginning. Good luck finding those. The same theory goes for large tortoise species.

Don't forget to covet your volunteers. No matter how weird or pushy they are, practice saying, "thank you." Volunteers can do more than just clean cages and walk dogs. They enthusiastically tell people about their favorite animals available for adoption. They also contribute valuable life skills.

Have volunteers drive, teach, fundraise, do home inspections and yes, even write. They can compile mailing lists, build shelters, fix vehicles, give tours . . . Remember, without volunteers you have to do everything yourself. There is never enough time for that at any shelter.

By the way, if you feel that only you can care for the animals properly or you need to do it all yourself, you're just one teensy-weensy step shy of becoming the definition of an animal hoarder. Don't open a rescue!

Another consideration for your rescue will be how to go about placing animals. This is far more in-depth than hanging up an adoptions sign. What sort of applicants do you hope to recruit? Who will inspect the homes and when? Follow up on adoptions? Did you evaluate all animals involved for compatibility with other pets in the prospective home? Children? Teens? Males? Swimming pools? Loud dishwashers? Fear of floor tile? Funny? Yes. But, I am not kidding.

And finally, who is going to manage your membership program and publish your newsletter? A good membership program keeps you at the front of people's minds when they are looking to adopt, making out donation checks, wanting to attend an event . . . A great mailing list is like great sex. It should deliver multiple positive results every time! Sorry, guys. Deal with it!

Okay. I think we've touched on the minimum considerations for founding your nonprofit animal sanctuary. "Wait a minute, Nola, you ninny," you might be thinking. "How do I find the animals that need rescuing? You didn't cover that, you satirical, yet gorgeous, and brilliant, dream-stomping bitch."

Thank you! Actually, I didn't need to cover the hands-on act of animal rescuing. You are about to meet every half-baked neonate who ever bought a kitten they didn't realize would eventually have a bowel movement. They'll start dumping their responsibilities on your step the moment your first fence goes up. It won't matter if the sign out front says, "Dyslexic, Orange-Spotted, Tree Frogs Sanctuary."

Follow up: If my article inspired you to learn more about founding your own sanctuary, then you weren't paying attention. Nonetheless, if you would like to learn more, the good folks at Best Friends Animal Society offer an excellent workshop for you. How to Start an Animal Sanctuary is an intensive, week-long class overflowing with specific details and considerations necessary for getting your non-profit shelter off on the right paw. I have attended the workshop myself and highly recommend it for anyone working in this business, or considering starting their own animal rescue. Visit www.bestfriends.org to learn more.

25% of dog owners in the United States own two dogs; 12% own three or more.

Nola Lee Kelsey

Flipper's Guide to the Hollydaze

My name is Flipper and I'm spozed to remind all the puppies out there that people set aside daze now and then where they act even weirder than usual. These daze are called Hollydaze. On Hollydaze humans toss their normal (if'n you can call 'em that) routines out the dog door, choosing instead to act extra funny. I think it has something to do with that hole I chewed in the basement gas line. But, I ain't forsures on that.

For the first year or two these silly behaviors can confuse young pups. Frankly, I don't care. But, my Mom told me 'cause I speak puppy, I should document some of my favorite Hollydaze, so other dogs know what to expect. I don't like any of them Hollydaze too much. But, Mom writes everything, so what else would she want me to do?

Oh well, I guess as long as I need a disposable thumb to turn that old can opener of ours, I'm kinda stuck. No write, no food. So I haves to do what I am told and these are what people hollydaze mean to all you young pups out there.

Christmas

Your people will kill a tree and bring its body inside the house. They'll stand it up, but they expect you not to pee on it. So make sure they're not looking when you do. They'll even decorate the dead tree and windows with glowing candies. Heads up! They electrocute the candy so you'll die if'n you take a taste.

Next your family will pile stacks of shiny, wrapped boxes under the pee tree. They'll probably say you can't play with them. I don't understand why they taunt us so. Just when you can't take it anymore, one morning everyone wakes up and plays with the boxes no one was supposed to play with. People sometimes suck.

Easter

Mom boils up lots of yummy eggs. Next all the short people in the family soak them in pretty colors while splashing the smelly dye all over the table and floor so they match the eggs. Last time I put a yellow spot that big on the floor, I got in trouble.

After a couple days the eggs start to get stinky. Dad doesn't like the stink either. He usually steals the eggs and hides them all over the yard, so no one will find 'em all.

Later, when the little people notice the eggs missing, they put on fancy clothes just to go look for the smelly eggs. I don't think their noses work very well, but don't sniff them out or eat them yourself or you'll get into more trouble. The scariest part of this holiday is that they dip rabbits in Chocolate and bite their heads off. I keep my ears down for three weeks prior, just to make sure there ain't no mistakes.

Thanksgiving

I just don't get it. Family comes in from all over the country just to eat. They must not have much food in other places. I spoze we're lucky. All the women cook more food than you could possibly imagine. They make the whole house smell like heaven. Dad tells me I don't need to beg for everything. Yet the others act surprised when I hop up on the table and just help myself.

Halloween

This one is definitely not going to make any sense to you puppies. You kinda have to see Halloween for yourself to believe it's real. Near as I can tell people disguise themselves, so they won't be recognized when they go around robbing their neighbors. The stupid neighbors keep opening the door no matter how much people steal.

Last year my brother Jerry disguised me as Dorothy from the Wizard of Oz. Then he dressed up as Toto. Seems silly since I'm already a terrier. Oh well, we stole lots of cookies and never got caught. Except when we robbed mean Mrs. Ferguson from next door. She had apples. Yuck!

The funniest part of Halloween is that people cut up squash and then light the inside on fire. If you pee through the holes just right you can put the fire out. I got four last year. Then one of my Dorothy braids caught fire. Two daze later, Mom made the pee squash into pies. That was the one time I didn't steal any food.

Fourth of July

I can't stand to think of it. This is the worst hollydaze ever! War breaks out all over town, shots are fired and the sky begins to fall. Why would people schedule such a thing? Maybe it's some sort of ritualized retaliation for all the theft that takes place on Halloween.

Whenever possible you should run away from home as soon as you hear the first shots. You can't count on your people to save you. My zombie-assed family just stands there staring up at the falling missles and chants, "Ooo, Ahhhh, Oh". I think it's called PTSD or PMS or something. When all else fails hide under the couch.

One thing you should know, a similar battle, complete with explosions, takes place at exactly midnight on something called New Year's Eve, but it doesn't last too long. Luckily, everyone gets too drunk to fight much. And if'n they turn their backs on the punch bowl, so do I!

That's all I have to say about that.

Seventy percent of dogfighters or other animal abuse offenders have also been arrested for violent crimes against people. Often those who abuse people start out abusing animals, then escalate. All of society suffers the consequences when animal abuse is ignored. It's not just a problem for animal lovers.

Nola Lee Kelsey

A Curiously Early Lodge Dog Christmas

"It is a fair, even-handed, noble adjustment of things, that while there is infection in disease and sorrow, there is nothing in the world so irresistibly contagious as laughter and good-humor."

- - A Christmas Carol, Charles Dickens

The unsuspecting snowman had no idea what perils awaited him. He simply sat there, grinning away on the back of my golf cart. Clueless! Christmas came early this year to the Land of Misfit Dogs. The role of Santa would be mine! The role of clueless befell the snowman.

129

A half hour earlier I had plowed into Dogtown's
staff room in my usual chipper mood, fully prepared
to choke the life out of the coffee maker if it did not
produce quickly. What maniacal fiend had delivered
giant boxes for me to lug around so early in the day?

Could anything possibly come out of Wyoming
that I'd want in my life at 7:45 a.m.? Why were they
addressed to, "The Dogs at The Lodges?" Wielding a
large kitchen knife I gleefully stabbed into the first box.
Coffee perked rhythmically in the background.

To my surprise dozens of plush toys erupted from
every box. As I sliced the tape which bound them
inside, reindeers, angels, snowmen, tin soldiers and the
like pushed upward, overflowing onto the floor.
Within moments I sat in a giant pile of stuffed toys.
How could I not smile? The unexpected bounty of fun
ignited a feeling of Christmas despite the heat of the
desert in July.

Apparently a business in Casper, Wyoming had
held a "stuffed animal drive" for the dogs. It was a
simple act of kindness. Even more amazing, two young
children, eight year old twin sisters, had donated many

of their own toys. The last of the boxes contained the girls' letters.

"Dear Best Friends,

I want to give your dogs one of my stuffed animals because we had a garage sail and I still have some left. These are the dogs I want to give the stuffed animals to.

Sophie,
Orea,
Shelby, and
Fillbert
I hope the dogs like them see ya soon!

Yor Friend
M. R."

"Dear Best Friends,

I would like you to give my stufft animals to these dogs Quick Draw, Valeatine, Kima and Daja. What ever Stofft animals are left over please give all the rest of the dogs. Give all the dogs a hug for me. Thank you!

Sincery,
H. R."

There certainly would be enough "stofft animals" left for all. While piling toys into my staff golf cart for distribution, its growing resemblance to a sleigh became undeniable. The ramshackle old cart mirrored that of Dr. Seuss' Grinch Who Stole Christmas much more than it resembled Santa's high-class ride. For a moment I glanced around looking for a small dog to strap tree branch antlers on, but there was no time to waste. There was a cart full of cheer to deliver.

As I made my appointed rounds, The Lodges became a "Bah Humbug" free zone. Pure joy erupted in every run. The "Lodges" area of Best Friends is where dogs needing to be housed singly or in twos live. There are certain advantages to being a Lodge Dog. Without a pack to fight with, cookies and toys can be distributed with ease. For the Lodge Dogs this day would be packed full of extra play. For me it suddenly became about unbridled silliness!

Who could have dreamed that so many of the animals would react with such unadulterated joy from a simple new toy? Everywhere merriment took over. Even the idlest dogs morphed, becoming like children on Christmas morning. Each played with the gifts in their own special way. Some tossed their toys skyward and twirled them around, like a scene from the Nut Cracker, accentuated with dust and drool. Others rolled on them, flopping gracelessly on their backs like fish out of water. Several trotted in circles proudly showing their present off to the world. "Look what I got!"

Tex surprised me most of all. This big hound mix stands as tall as a sleigh and his coat glows as red as Rudolf's nose. My choice was obvious. I'd give him his own reindeer toy. Tex's tough-guy image melted away. First his new stuffy received a tender bath of sloppy kisses. Next it was tucked softly under his chin for safe keeping. Later, as afternoon rains darkened the sky, Tex gently carried his toy into his lodge. Together they napped for hours side by side. For my precious Tex, I had chosen wisely.

Truth be told, in every case I took my toy selection duties much too seriously. Dahlila, The Lodges' unofficial princess mascot, had to have the cheerleader teddy bear and for Valentine something pink, of course. Whitney, the brindle pit, always loves frogs. Who knows why?

As for Meatball (a.k.a. The Meat Head), Caregiver Mike suggested the biggest, silliest, stuffed bunny was a must for the biggest, silliest, rottweiler to ever grace our universe. The absurd site of this floppy-eared duo, with identical facial expressions, brought tears of laughter to my eyes. It was another perfect match.

Admittedly my darker side selected the dog who would receive a toy resembling a certain traveling gnome. Zeus! The gnome must go to Zeus. No doubt the gnome would meet a quick and decisive end. The forlorn looking Zeus's primary joy in life is disemboweling stuffed toys. That thought provided me immense satisfaction.

To me, the gnome represented every airport security guard to ever rifle through my underwear. Within seconds the gnome's head traveled westward. His left foot took flight in the direction of Denver. Stuffing coated the run like new-fallen snow. Zeus and I were both quite satisfied.

As for the snowman? It was with an equally twisted mindset that I tossed the smirking menace in with Deja – a lanky, wolf-like, giant of a dog. Despite my glee at playing Santa, the snowman's grin vexed me a tad. Yet, much to my dismay, the carrot-nosed doll emerged victorious! Deja played with his new toy most of the morning, yet caused no harm.

As my shift ended they both sat in Deja's dog yard looking quite pleased with themselves. I had to giggle. Just like Tex, Deja also proved himself to be a gentle giant. Deja vu! It would appear that I, not the snowman, had been the clueless one. Of course, I had never gotten to my morning coffee.

Few words are adequate to describe the happiness brought to the Lodge Dogs that day. Be it tossing toys around rambunctiously or carrying one off for a nap, this was a whimsical diversion from their routine – something new. You could literally feel the dogs' spirits lift ever higher. Watching these antics was both a privilege and a curiously early miracle. To think, the magic of this early Christmas cheer was given by a caring group of strangers, two selfless kids and a slow "yard sail." Simple acts of kindness know no bounds. Here's hoping we all capture that spirit throughout every New Year!

Nola Lee Kelsey

Based on the ASPCA's rates for treatment, Ibuprofen is the number one cause of dog poisonings.

Nola Lee Kelsey

The Night Before A Dogtown Christmas

Twas the night before Christmas, and all through Best Friends,

Not a creature was stirring, except a few hens;

The stockings were hung way up high in the air,

In hopes that no goat kids would give them a tear;

The cats each were nestled all snug in their beds,

While visions of families danced in their heads;

And dogs in their lodge runs, and I in my Jeep,

Had just settled down for some much needed sleep,

When out by some cactus arose such a clatter,

I sprang from my rest to see what was the matter.

Away to the front lot I flew like a flash,

Tripped over the sidewalk and slipped near the trash.

The moon on the breast of the new-blown sand,

Gave the luster of mid-day to objects at hand,

When, what to my sunburned eyes should appear,

But a sleigh full of puppies flying quite near,

The little old rescuer landed so quick,

I knew in a moment he must be St. Nick.

More rapid than beagles his coursers they came,

And he smiled, and nodded, and called them by name;

"Now, Dachsie! now, Dobie! now, Tootsie and Muffy!

On, Comet! on, Cotton! on, Dudley and Fluffy!

To the top of the steps! Cross the lobby with all!

Now bounce along! Pounce along! Trounce along all!"

Into the clinic the vet team did fly,

Where they examined each puppy, not pondering why,

Then up to New Friends the trainers they flew,

With the sleigh full of puppies, and St. Nicholas too.

While I worked making ready, I heard on our roof

The prancing and pawing of each reindeer hoof.

As I filled bowls with water, and was turning around,

Through a swamp cooler St. Nicholas came with a bound.

He was dressed in faux fur, from his head to his knee,

And his clothes were all soaking with drool and pup wee;

The wiggling puppies he had brought in his sack,

And he looked like a Caregiver just handling his pack.

His eyes -- how they twinkled! His dimples quite funny!

His cheeks were like roses, his nose like a bunny!

His droll little mouth would speak first just to give

Thanks to Best Friends abandoned puppies may live;

Nola Lee Kelsey

The top of a poop scoop he held tight in his hand,
"I'll clean a few dog runs while here in your land;"
The pups had broad faces and little round bellies,
That shook when they wrestled like cups of fruit jellies.

They were chubby and plump, a good sign of health,
And I laughed at their kisses, in spite of myself;
A dip of their eyes and a nod of their heads,
Soon gave me to know they needed their beds;

I spoke not a word, but went back to my work,
And fluffed all their blankets; my own little quirk,
St. Nick returned tired, with a weepy red nose,
And giving a nod, to the rooftop he rose;

He sprang to his sleigh, with his volunteer whistle,
And that sleigh flew away like the down of a thistle.
But I heard Santa say, as he vanished from sight,
"Find new homes for them all, Best Friends does that right!"

142

Follow up: *The Night Before a Dogtown Christmas* is now available as a children's book, illustrated by Avonelle Kelsey, owner of the Kelsey Gallery of Fine Arts in Hot Springs, South Dakota. This whimsical take on a holiday classic may be ordered through your favorite bookstore or online retailer.

Nola Lee Kelsey

Paul McCartney recorded an ultrasonic whistle, audible to dogs, but not people, at the end of the Beatles' song, "A Day in the Life." This was for the amusement of his Shetland sheepdog.

Nola Lee Kelsey

10 Signs of a Stupid Dog

Wars have broken out over what to name a family pet. In fact, you may be astonished to learn that there were no weapons of mass destruction in Iraq. Surprise! Bush was actually trying to secure America's control over the global supply of rare pet name books published in ancient Mesopotamia. The bulk of these books are rumored to be hidden in a cave near Iraq's border with Iran. So, obviously we'll have to invade them next.

Closer to home, marital relations have terminated for less important matters than what to name a kitten or pet guppy. Personally I could never walk down the aisle towards any man who doesn't see that Alfonso is the perfect guppy name. And, should I ever own the perfect guppy, Alfonso will be his name. What I had in mind for my own puppy's name was something that reflected my persona. Family bylaws require this.

My astronomy buff brother once had a dog named Comet. My sword fighting brother named one of his cats some unpronounceable German word meaning One Who Stabs. My older sister names many of her dogs Pee On, which bears an unfortunate resemblance to how she treats many of her company's employees. My younger brother? He has no pets and also no pet names. Coincidences? I think not. As for my kid sister, she has a dog named Tootsie. Of course that has no real connection to my point, so I thought I'd mention it.

In naming my puppy Koko I proudly opted for branding myself an elitist bio nerd. She was named after Koko the Gorilla, The Gorilla Foundation's world-renowned, sign language speaking, kitten loving, prestigious primate. My fervent hope was that Koko the Dog would grow up to be as friendly, beautiful and intelligent as her revered gorilla counterpart.

Alas, as they say, two out of three ain't bad. It took a while to admit it, but my little girl is never going to be the canine poster child for interspecies communication. How do I know? Let's not talk about her here.

On an unrelated note, the following are ten surefire signs someone else's dog (not mine) isn't the brightest bulb in the chandelier.

1) Tries to shake herself dry while she is still in the water

2) Gets lost inside the dog door

3) Breaks the mirror trying to sniff the butt of dog that bears a striking resemblance to herself

4) Thought a vote for Bush would give her more landscaping to piss on (If only!)

5) Eats the mail, but fetches the mailman

6) Needs GPS to find her bones in the yard – NOTE: they are not buried

7) Will enthusiastically chase a butterfly straight off a cliff, even if no actual butterfly is around

8) Fell for that whole pork being the other white meat thing

9) Compulsively chases the tail on dad's good tux (no matter that it's hanging perfectly still in the back of his closet)

10) Can't help mom think of a 10th thing on her stupid dog list

Yes indeed, if your dog (not mine) shows any of these tendencies you might want to try a guppy next time. Perhaps it would be best if people named their dogs after the dog's personality traits, not their own human quirks. Chubby, for a plump chow chow, or Happy for a wiggle-butt dog makes more sense. You certainly couldn't go more wrong than naming Koko the dimwitted dog after a gorilla with a larger vocabulary than your average reality TV star.

Before being evacuated to America, my dog Flipper was named by the staff at Beirut for the Ethical Treatment of Animals (B.E.T.A.). You see his front feet point outward, forming a perfect dolphin tail shape. (For those of you under 30, Flipper was a TV show dolphin that rescued people who had lost their ability to survive outdoors due to excessive text messaging).

Hey, wait a minute! Flip was rescued during the 06 conflict between Hezbollah and Israel. Middle Eastern conflict does net America great dog names. Who needs oil? That G.W. Bush is a stone cold genius.

Nola Lee Kelsey

Considered the Royal Dog of Egypt, the Saluki is recognized as the oldest breed in the world, dating back as far back as 329 B.C.

Nola Lee Kelsey

South Dakota:
Breed Ban Pierces Heart of the Heartland

I'll admit to having more than a bit of trouble writing this story. My original assignment was to write a brief report for a web site. 'Just the facts ma'am.' Even back then the story kept morphing itself into a full book chapter, not a tight little web article. Brevity has never been my forte and a breed ban in my own back yard – the State of South Dakota - definitely provided me with enough ammo for a thousand satires. But, here you have it.

The rumors are true. Leola, South Dakota, has indeed, tragically, passed Breed Specific Legislation, banning certain 'types' of dogs in their town. A summary of the law's details are as follows:

- The breeds involved are pit bulls, bull mastiffs, Rottweilers, Doberman pinschers, German shepherds, and any mixes of those breeds.

- Dogs of those breeds already registered to town residents are "grandfathered" in and not subject to the ban.

- According to Mayor Dean Schock, whom I interviewed for this story, if there is a question of lineage in suspected mixed breed 'offenders,' a genetic test will be conducted.

- The town council originally passed the ban. Later a local person adopted a Rottweiler puppy, and had the law put before voters in an effort to keep the pup. The town's citizens supported the legislation by a vote of 103 – 27. The puppy's fate was not as easily determined.

- On a more progressive note, Leola does require all dogs to be fixed unless a breeding license is obtained, so puppies will not be born to the banned breeds.

Those of us who work with shelter dogs understand, or have access to information on, the innumerable flaws of breed bans. We know the science does not play out. We know this seemingly 'easy out' ultimately causes more harm than good. So, I will not dive into that here. I will, however, briefly touch on some less spoken of points.

There was no preemptive incident, such as a dog attack, that spurred the town into reactionary legislation. Leola's residents were simply worried that with children, joggers and bicyclists around town a breed ban was needed to ensure safety. The town folks requested the ban. Like most who understand the flaws and heartbreak of breed bans, my blood was boiling at the legislation's passing, but upon hearing of citizens actually asking government to take away an individual freedom my blood ran cold.

Immediately I wanted to hire a helicopter and drop leaflets over the community. They would say, "Ban Chains, Not Breeds!", "Fence in Your Yards, Not Your Liberties" or "Bad Owners Make Aggressive Dogs!" Lucky for Leola the high cost of gas kept me grounded. Grrr!

Readers may have noted the extremely odd presence of German shepherds on the list of banned breeds in Leola. According to Mayor Schock, a friend of his, who once worked with police dogs in Aberdeen, SD, had heard of an incident in which someone adopted a retired police dog and there was an attack. Wow, how kind of the Mayor to illustrate a point for me.

Are you kidding? Is this the kind of airtight scientific evidence Americans want laws based on? This third party, partial account of a one in a million shot, leading to outlawing an entire breed is the ultimate testimonial as to what happens once these dangerous flood gates are opened. If I mention to the Mayor that my sister's dog attacked me when I was eight, would Pomeranians be next on Leola's hit list?

That shot fired, I have to say, Mayor Schock was a very accommodating victim of my interview style. He was gracious, well-spoken and intelligent (German shepherd thing not withstanding). Let us not hate the town of Leola. Let us hate the lack of education on the subject of dog behavior, dog breeds and animal abuse that is the ultimate cause of this Breed Specific Legislation. (That and a hearty helping of human sloth.)

Preaching, tirades and name calling will not help the dogs of my state. And the dogs will need your help! Practice kindness in educating the Mayor and his town. Share your knowledge. Why? Because other communities in South Dakota have contacted Mayor Schock wanting copies of Leola's B.S. Legislation for their own community's use. I occasionally wonder how those phone calls go.

"Hi, this is the Secretary over in Townville. We heard about your dog breed ban. Our citizens don't really appear interested in preventing problem dogs by preventing animal cruelty or being responsible pet owners. Could we get a copy

of your law, so that their individual freedoms may be flushed down the toilet instead?"

"Sure, no problem. What's your fax number? While you're on the phone, we also have a law we're working on that bans chains, a major cause of dog aggression. Would you like a copy of that as well?"

"Nope. That's a bit too logical for Townville. Besides, I own a share of the feed mill that sells the chains here in our area. However I did hear that a falling coconut killed a man in Malaysia last year, when he was walking his dachshund. Do you have any bills in the works that ban dachshunds and palm trees?

"Boy, howdy, we will now!"

Yup! Impending regional tragedy has been unleashed. If we can't convince citizens of the Heartland to protect their treasured freedoms, how can we win against big governments?

A Final Thought
To the people of Leola: Love Dogs! Hate Dogs! It makes no difference. This is also about responsibility,

basic freedom and setting a dangerous precedent for government and law enforcement, which will be open to all forms of abuse.

Hold people to their obligations to raise animals that are not prone to aggression in the first place. (No chains, no cruelty, spay / neuter . . .) Hold all levels of government to the highest standards when protecting rights of individual Americans. Once police can enter our homes and kill our pets on suspicion of a lineage, there are few lines the government will not be able to justify crossing. Don't let fear erode your Freedom. Find a better way!

A Final Final Thought

A study by the Centers for Disease Control, "Which Dogs Bite?" found that chained dogs are 2.8 times more likely to bite. The dogs most likely to bite are male, unneutered, and chained. Neither 'unneutered' or 'chained' is a breed. They are human failings. Any dog can become aggressive if the owner is irresponsible.

City of Leola
602 3rd St
Leola, SD 57456

Nola Lee Kelsey

In 2008, Gerda Verburg, the Dutch Minister of
Agriculture, informed Parliament that the rule banning
pit bulls in the Netherlands would be lifted.
The fifteen year old law was found to be ineffective.
If entire countries with years of experience get it,
why doesn't the American Government
learn from them?

Nola Lee Kelsey

What's that Mutt?

Guessing the heritage of mutts is a competitive art form among shelter workers. Keepers, caregivers and vet techs stand around scratching their chins and nodding in deep contemplation. You'd think we were trying to unravel the square root of the DaVinci Code or identify the last three of the Cornel's savory eleven herbs and spices. Self-proclaimed experts would sooner die than admit to each other that we often can't tell the lineage of mixed breed dogs based on their appearance.

Nonetheless, shelter paperwork often demands we commit to stray dogs being primarily just one or two breeds. "He's a Dobbie mix." "She's a Dalmatian, Pug cross." Wilbur the stray must never be listed as the obvious Aussie-Lahpsa-Cocker-Shitza-Ainu-Poo-Poo he is. There is simply not enough room on the intake form. A primary breed must be declared at all costs to reality. The debate can get ugly.

"Well, those are obviously Cocker Spaniel feet."

"Yes, but look at the poodle hair."

"That's not poodle hair. It's blue merle in color. Your hair is poodle hair."

"My hair isn't blue, you ninny."

"I never said it was."

"Well then, he's obviously a Samoyed cross."

"What?"

"Oh, just put Border Collie mix on the form. Who are we kidding? This mutt will put in for social security before we agree on the breed."

"Fine. Your comb over is starting to slip anyway."

"My comb over is not blue!"

This same conversation takes place daily at shelters and sanctuaries all over the world. It's just one of a million ways people overanalyze dogs.

Even though I have never seen a single Thai Ridgeback running loose in the United States, her mutt-ly offspring are reported on intake forms in all fifty states. They are as common as poodle mixes (many of whom are actually bichon frise crosses). Yet no one I know has ever encountered a designer Thai-Poo (not to be mistaken with Tae Bo). In fact, the only place you don't hear of Thai ridgeback mixes is in Thailand.

We see in dogs traits from the breeds each of us are most familiar with. After being around canines too long, we also see those traits in each other. Hence phrases like: "His new wife has the nose of a Schnauzer" or "That man has all the charisma of a comatose coon hound."

Speaking of which, I'd like to wish a happy and hearty, hello to the gentleman who hit on me at the coffee kiosk last week. Here's hoping the drink you ordered was heavily caffeinated.

Truth is, dogs are likely to look like their ancestral region's traits. That is why Great Pyrenees resemble snow-capped mountains, Irish Setters have red hair, and America is a melting pot of mutts.

Fortunately, mystery-mutt lineages can now be unraveled, thanks to the good people who brought us science. Several companies are now decoding the genetic identities of mutts. Just hop online and order your Mutt-Decoder kit for $65.00. Collect a DNA sample from inside the mouth of your shelter's newfound, terrified, frothing stray and in mere weeks the mystery will be solved. And you can finish up your intake paperwork. How cool is that?

Just for fun, I've sent a genetic sample in for my probable Aussie poo cross, Henry. Vegas odds makers doubt my expertise. They have him at 20 to 1 in favor of a designer Thai ridgeback, blue comb-over cross.

The oldest living dog ever recorded was a Queensland Heeler named Bluey, who lived to the ripe old age of 29 years and 5 months.

Nola Lee Kelsey

How to Choose the Wrong Pet Sitter

I've been an animal lover since I was born, I think.
Those first few hours are a bit fuzzy. It is a cruel streak
of nature that I was also born with an insatiable
passion for travel.

One of the most overwhelming issues dog parents
face is how to grab any time away, well enough the
minimum six weeks of shoestring travel I need just to
feel my skin fit again. Hominid children can get
passports. Dogs only get quarantined. Worse still, dogs
have to ride in the luggage compartment. Children,
sadly, can not be checked. Heaven knows which lost

baggage department Rover will eventually turn up in. Yet, airlines are quick to return lost kids, no matter where their parents hide.

All this puts innocent travel junkies at the mercy of pet sitters. Choosing the right sitter is vital. How do I know this? Easy! I've never hired a good sitter. I've spent years cultivating the science of selecting some of the worst pet nannies ever produced. Hence, I am an expert at how not to choose a good one.

My first pet sitter I discovered by scrupulously searching my kitchen. He is my son. It's been a long time since he got married and moved away, but as I recall his name was, Larry or Jerry or Barry or . . . Whatever.

Anyway, at the time, LarryJerry was a teenager and competitive kick boxer. While this sounds like an obvious recipe for house sitting disaster, I assure you I've done worse. In retrospect, at least I knew JerryBarry cherished his dogs.

When I traveled I could rest easy knowing that my wine collection might vanish, the garage might implode and my home would probably looked like a flop house for homeless pizza delivery boys, but the pets would safe. After all, they had a live-in bodyguard capable of disemboweling a leopard with a single kick if one happened to wander in front of the television set. I should have recognized this then as pet sitting Nirvana.

At seventeen BarryLarry moved to Thailand to practice kicking things at a new longitude. Meanwhile, back at home, I began to suffocate. Deprived of airline security seizing my explosive pink foam hair rollers, depression set in. Without the rush of adrenalin and carbon monoxide that only third world taxi rides can elicit, I started to pace like a caged polar bear. I must travel or die!

How could I afford to hire a pet sitter and to travel? Then in a stroke of faux-genius, or cerebral collapse, I ran a newspaper advertisement for a dog nanny. "Free room with shared kitchen and bath in exchange for taking care of my animals when I travel." It seemed like a good idea at the time.

I visualized taking flight without a care in the world, while Julie Andrews ran my Dalmatians through a field of wildflowers. "The hills are alive . . ."

What I got was more like Axel Rose, only not as considerate of others. Enter Rodger.

Rodger took up residence on my living room couch faster than Darfur refugees can swarm a complimentary buffet. Apparently the "shared kitchen and bath" concept eluded Rodger. Even when I held my advertisement upside-down and squinted at it through a bottle of Corona, I could not make out the words, "Wanted, living room nester!"

Blocked from the central hub of my home, there was no way to escape the relentless onslaught of basketball games and basketball games. But my travel plans were being set. I was hesitant to speak up and risk jolting Rodger into a state of consciousness, lest he might escape.

In all fairness to Rodger he did take the dogs snowshoeing once. It must have been half time. During this brief outing every small forest creature with a pulse ascended upon my pack. Once the skunk smell settled down, getting the porcupine quills out of eight dogs proved to be more exhilarating than backing a pickup truck over my own spleen.

Anyway, late one night as the LA Lakers vs. the PA Bakers or whatever, echoed under my bedroom door, I tried desperately not to think about the bathroom being on the other side of the living room, or about having to go pee. We all know how well that works.

After layering on several pairs of pajamas, bath robes and a trench coat to preserve some sense of modesty in front of the dog nanny, I set forth for the bathroom. Three steps from my bedroom door, the image of Rodger pleasuring himself on my couch seared into my retinas for all eternity.

He was in my living room, on my couch, watching my TV, jollying himself up. My remote was in one hand, Little Rodger in the other. Surely he noticed me bolt like lightning back into my room, yet to his credit I am pretty sure he finished the job at hand. I know he finished the basketball game.

Meanwhile, I sat cornered like a rat with an exploding bladder, praying for the Angel of Death to take one of us before breakfast. At 1 a.m. I climbed out my own bedroom window. And despite being a home owner, I wandered through the darkness, seeking out a place to pee in the alley behind my own storage building. Travel the world? Hell no! I never even got to the movies before evicting Jolly Rodger.

Hindsight would soon dictate that I should have tossed Rodger three remote control batteries, a half gallon of KY and headed for the airport. Hindsight is Latin for Candi. Enter Candi.

Candi had no eyebrows. On days she went to work she drew them on. On days she stayed home I suppressed an overwhelming desire to duct tape a level to her forehead so I could try and even them up. In my own defense, Candi had been forced upon me.

While working graveyard shifts at a local convenience store, my boss, a rigid shrew-like woman, rang me up. "Nola, we have the nicest gal here. We want to hire her but she needs a place to stay while she relocates to the area." The phone bill containing Jolly Rodger's $75.00 call to Tel Aviv had just arrived.

"Thanks Shrew, but I am kinda roommated out at the moment." Shrew was adamant. Stunned that my boss would put me in such a position, I summoned my courage. I stalled - courageously. "Ah, I, ah, um, I'll think about it."

Early the next morning my life was shanghaied. Candi introduced herself at the store. Her eyebrows were within centimeters of being evenly sketched, giving off a mild illusion of sanity. Enter Shrew; they tag teamed me.

I should explain myself here. I was fully aware that, "while she relocates to the area" was also Latin. It translates as: "does not have two dimes to rub on her missing eyebrows, let alone have the money it would take to get into an apartment of her own."

Yet, we all know that same old story. You want to travel and you have a son, GarryBarry, to put through Muay Thai camp. Why is it that parents never seem to put aside enough money to lay the foundations for a good Ultimate Fighting education? Anyway, you can't afford to upset your boss, so you bring home extra work. I brought browless Candi home to meet the dogs.

For a week Candi was the perfect roommate. We were on opposite schedules at the store. My dogs had company day and night and we saw very little of each other. We'd touch base when I drove her to work after my shift. Candi, of course, had no car. I'd awaken for work when the taxi brought her home.

By week two, I noted my new roomy liked a cold beer as much as me. By week three, I noted she also liked warm beer, Goldshlager, Schnapps, Vodka, Jack Daniels, Cuervo and seconds of Goldshlager significantly more than me. Sometimes she'd mix them.

Strange but true, my zoo's new nanny could afford to drink liquor laced with 24-carat gold shavings until Candi tossed her cookies. Yet, getting her to kick in money for gas or utilities was like trying to extract blood from an eighty proof turnip. Priorities, I guessed.

By week five, I would come home and simply step over her unconscious body on my kitchen floor. So would the dogs. I'd pull the sharp knife from the raw steak meat piled up on my countertop, then contemplate the danger this posed to my pets and go to bed. If she could afford to leave steak out for the zoo, so be it!

At week six, I tossed her out on her Candy-coated ass. A bottle of Goldshlager cushioned her landing.

Shrew let her dissatisfaction with me be known. How could I be so cruel to this poor hapless waif?

Once admonished for trying to help out both Shrew and Candi, a lesser woman might have sought revenge for her boss behaving so unprofessionally. After all, Shrew had overstepped the bounds of a boss and put me in an awkward situation. But, I'm not vengeful. I'm mature. I'll never mention her extramarital relations with the manager at one of our other stores. No sir, not me. I simply switched jobs.

Besides, karma kicked in. Just weeks after Candi somehow landed her own apartment; the local district attorney began investigating her for stealing from the store. Shrew's store. Taxis, liquor, steak, an apartment…? Oh yea, I get it now. At least I could not find a worse dog sitter. Why not try another advertisement? Enter Ernest.

I suspected Ernest was somewhat mentally handicapped. But how do you ask someone that? Hey, um, I was wondering, if, um, are you a tad bit retarded or what? All I knew was he got a monthly check from the government and was not the quickest fish lapping the pond. No worries! He was magnificent with my dogs! Hallelujah!

Ernest related to my animals on their own level. He and Dusty, my retriever, would enthusiastically play and wrestle together. Then, they would both chase my Aussie shepherds around the yard for hours on end. Kindred spirits came to mind. Say it again! Hallelujah!

I was off to Asia for a over a month. Faster than I could get to my favorite Bangkok day-spa, memories of Rodger the couch masturbator and Candi the inebriated klepto cashier drained from my body. For weeks I replenished my soul via regular infusions of scuba, sand and sun. Third time's the charm. I was a genius at finding pet sitters!

Weeks later, I wandered back into my home, with a deep tan, a head full of Rasta braids, and wearing enough hemp jewelry to bridge the River Kwai. Laid back was an understatement more suited to Richard Simmons. The dogs were happy, well fed and all accounted for. The cats were still cats. Nirvana? Not quite.

All was not perfect. As the haze from jetlag and the occasional mushroom-stuffed omelet lifted, so did my blood pressure. My escape had not been without flaws. There were a few flies in the ointment. There were oodles of flies in the kitchen. You see Ernest had never taken the trash out while I was away. Did I mention I was gone for over a month? Happy Happy Joy Joy!

Not once had he even mopped up after my pack of mud-slogging pooches. My tropical vibe was vanquished by the five days of intense housework that welcomed me home. In all fairness, I never actually told Ernest to maintain the house above minimal HAZMAT standards. It seemed self-evident. But, the guy never washed a single dish while I was away. I'm not sure how he ate once all the dishes and flatware were collecting mold spores in the sink. I am sure I don't want to know.

It's not to say Ernest hadn't tossed stuff out. Though it was a blessing he never took the trash cans to the curb. This gave me time to retrieve my art supplies, family photos and other valuables he had put in the garbage. Why had he randomly tossed my personal belongings out? Well, my guess is it was because they would not fit into the kitchen sink.

None of this was as startling as the fact that when I pointed out to Ernest that his housekeeping shortcomings were bizarre, unfathomable and quite possibly stupid, he shrugged it off.

Again, he and Dusty, my retriever, would enthusiastically play and wrestled together. Then, they would both chase my Aussie shepherds around the yard for hours on end. Kindred spirits came to mind.

Soon I noticed the only time Earnest didn't play with the dogs was when he stared straight at me. This proved to be a disturbingly creepy 49% of the time. Optometrists will tell you people need to blink. I assure you, that is not the case.

Ernest would stare at me when I cooked, when I cleaned, when I ate, and when I watched TV. He stared as I tried to unearth my hard wood floors from the mop-free month. He stared while I mined his trash collection from my pantry. No way could I have ever have snuck off to pee behind my storage building with Unblinking Ernest around.

I lasted two weeks with the hair on the back of my neck standing at full eerie attention. Creepiness overcame me. My desire to be politically correct and accepting of the mentally handicapped, albeit obvious ax murderer, living under my roof collapsed. That is when I explained to the unblinking art plunderer the importance of being Ernest, anywhere but in my home.

After experiencing these three pillars of pet sitting, I half heartedly made a few shorter escapes. Once I hired a local twenty-something to stay overnights while I was on a long weekend. Predictably he did not stay over. He just fed and fled. This approach was akin to a doggy drive-by. I even tried hiring a good friend to stay over for two brief nights. Fourteen dead Mantella frogs later, we are no longer in touch. And the beat goes on.

In retrospect, anyone needing a room desperately enough to nanny for a pack of large deaf dogs has something generically wrong with them. The problem with retrospect is that the whole 'retro' part comes after the fact. Go figure! Turns out, I'd landed the perfect house sitter without ever trying. Damn, I'm good!

After a hellish year of living flightlessly, I was saved. Enter CarryLarry. We high-fived each other as we passed in the driveway. I was off to the airport and parts unknown. TerryBarry came home from Thailand to visit his dogs. It's important for families to spend this quality time together.

In preparation for his stay, I programmed Pizza Palace's phone number into speed dial. Next I placed the telephone, a cork screw and a box of condoms on top of my wine collection. Then I gleefully wrote a blank check to our local bail bondsman. My zoo was safe. I could relax. Nirvana!

Fewer than nine years after being founded, the Dog Rescue Center Samui transformed the entire 250 square kilometer island of Koh Samui into Thailand's only rabies-free zone.

Nola Lee Kelsey

Rescuers vs. Hoarders

The psychological disorder often referred to as 'animal hoarding' has not been studied nearly enough. Nationwide there are few resources for law enforcement officials to call on when wondering if they have a hoarding situation in their town. Indeed on the surface it may be hard to tell if a person is an Animal Rescuer or an Animal Hoarder.

Even at some nationally renowned rescues, the owners or managers have been known to sink into hoarding over time, blurring the lines even further. This scenario makes a misunderstood issue even more difficult to bring to the forefront. Well-meaning donors don't want to know, and don't want the world to know, that in the end the once-reputable organization they proudly bragged about sponsoring had floundered. They unwittingly sponsored a hoarding situation where animals suffered at the hands of would-be saviors.

Truly, animal hoarding is as hideous to see as it is unacceptable to joke about. But we must at least talk about the problem in order to better educate people. It is the only way to stop the suffering, not just of animals, but of the mentally ill hoarders. The fuzzy line between what is a rescuer and what is a hoarder must be clarified. So for anyone out there wondering some of subtle ways to tell the difference between rescuers and hoarders, I have compiled this list to refer to.

- While running to break up a Doberman fight, an experienced rescuer calmly thinks, did I leave the coffee pot on this morning? If the stitches take my entire lunch hour (again) the house will burn.

- While running to break up a Chihuahua fight, an overwhelmed animal hoarder stops to adopt three more dogs.

- In a rescuer's home, dog hair is considered a condiment.

- In a hoarder's home, sarcoptic mange mites are considered an appetizer.

- Rescuers have a dog barrier in their 4-wheel drive in order to keep animals safely in the back seat.

- Hoarders keep litter boxes on the floors of their pastel blue Gremlins in order to keep cat shit off their gas pedal.

- Rescuers swerve off the road and drool profusely at the sight of a good six foot privacy fence.

- Hoarders know they are the only ones who can properly take care of whatever is helplessly suffering behind that blasted six foot privacy fence.

- Rescuers agonize over their selection of pet food.

- Hoarders agonize over how they can afford to feed themselves.

- Rescuers don't mind when their foster pet hops up on the bed mattress to sleep.

- Hoarders sleep on a mattress of dead cats.

- A rescuer's home can be recognized by all the holes in the yard and the pet toys in the living room.

- A hoarder's home can be recognized by all the holes in the floor boards and the smell in the neighborhood.

- Rescuers immediately spay and neuter every animal they save, and others that pass too close.

- Hoarders eventually tell the miniature Poodle to quit humping the kittens living in the couch cushions.

- Rescuers often walk their dogs on leashes.

- Hoarders often lock their dogs on chains.

- Rescuers place their foster pets in life-long homes so they can move on to help another animal.

- Hoarders place their extra pets in closets, so they can fit another animal into the trailer.

- Rescuers spend ten plus hours per day helping animals find paths to better lives.

- Hoarders spend ten plus minutes per day getting feces out of their eye brows.

Now people should be better able to spot those subtle little differences between Animal Rescuers and Animal Hoarders. I hope this helps to make those virtually indistinguishable grey areas a little bit clearer for everyone.

Ninety-nine percent of puppies sold in pet stores come from puppy mills. What percentage of stores do you think admit to customers that the dogs they sell are from puppy mills?
Don't 'buy' the lie!

Nola Lee Kelsey

Creating a No Chew Zone

"I would have called you back but Skeeter ate my cell phone." My neighbor, Barbara, had a puppy. She did not have a land line. Had Barb needed to call 911, she'd need to do a series of chest compressions on Skeeter's clavicle, than speak into his left eye. Can you hear me now?

I felt her pain. My own dog, Koko, a rescued black lab, husky cross, was at the same stage. If I lingered too long in my kitchen, I would likely return to find Koko in my office looking nervous. There would be enough feathers scattered around the room to fill a futon. That worked out well. You see, coincidentally, my flattened futon has recently been in need of some added feathers.

By the time Koko was ten months old, migrating Canada Geese would spot the continual flow of feathers drifting out of my front door. On occasion, they'd overnight on my filing cabinet with the expectation of finding a mate.

The moment I stepped inside Barb's door, I started inventorying the problems. One of my favorite puppy faux pas is buying the dog a shoe-shaped chew toy and then leaving your own shoes on the floor. Pups can't tell a rawhide chew from a leather Birkenstock shoe and they don't distinguish Gucci labels from Poochi labels.

There are three general rules to protecting your belongings from the wandering mouths of teething pups. First, give dogs a bounty of 'legal' chewies. I personally keep enough dog toys around my home to stock Santa's warehouse. Kongs®, Hurley toys, quality dental chews, dog safe stuffed animals . . . Let the fluff fly!

There is an ancient saying I just made up. "Better to have the guts of a toy alligator aloft in the living room, than your previous year's tax records shit out in the backyard." Just rolls off the tongue like poetry, don't you think?

The second rule for lessening the menace of canine consumptionism is keeping your legal chews interesting. Rotate them so they are always new and exciting. Keep them clean and fresh. Provide a variety of mentally stimulating toys. From stuffing Kongs with decadent yummies to collecting a bevy of treat dispensing games, you'll be doing yourself several favors.

Not only will you deter the use of your bamboo table legs as eco friendly K9 tooth picks, but giving treats and games when you go to leave the house makes your departure more bearable, even rewarding. This will help curb the development of separation anxiety.

The third way to avoid mishaps is the most obvious. Thus, it is the one people do the least. If you don't want something chewed on, don't put it where a dog can chew on it. It kind of rolls off the brain like a monumental heap of obvious, don't you think?

Shut closets and side room doors, especially for the first seven or eight years of your puppy's life. Keep the kitchen counter clear. If your dog is bigger than the refrigerator, super glue the door shut or suspend meat from the chandelier with a bear bag and pulley. It's all perfectly simple.

No matter what your background with animals, when you choose to bring a new dog into your home, material possessions will be sacrificed. Keeping my futon on the top shelf of my closet proved a tad impractical. The geese were nesting up there.

While bitter apple and other such sprays may help protect some belongings, the occasional animal digs the taste. Once I even tried rubbing green curry on my bamboo chair legs to deter Koko. It worked. Of course Flipper is Lebanese. He immediately erected a base camp under the table and was last seen ordering out for some olive oil. I haven't seen my cell phone since.

A dog's owner or handler most often is responsible for making a dog into a dangerous animal.

Any dog, regardless of breed, can be turned into a dangerous dog, just like any car with a moron at the wheel can become a dangerous car. Why do we ban breeds and not specific automotive models?

Nola Lee Kelsey

*Another Inconvenient Truth

The volunteers in front of me stalled at the gate. I could not comprehend why. Had a hole in the space time continuum engulfed them? It sucks when this happens. Time simply stood still.

The gate was open. The dogs, Veronica and Dagwood, were more than thrilled to be going on a walk. For once no escaped bulls were grazing on the path; at least that I could see. And yes, I definitely felt it when I pinched myself. But the volunteers were motionless.

Excited Dagwood pulled forward. The couple stood their ground. Had there been some mistake? Sometimes when newbies arrived at Three Springs to volunteer, they preferred to brush dogs or sit in the Cat House. Still the young couple had arrived with leashes, tennis shoes, water bottles and all the other typical trappings of dog walkers.

The dogs tried again to exit the run. Just when I was deciding between asking if they preferred to poop scoop or calling a tow truck to hoist their asses out of my area, the truth hit me. They were "Millaners." Crap!

To be clear, Millaners are not a sweet and tasty cookie product. Those are Milanos. Millaners are a product of television. Yes, the young couple in question were zealot-like, faux-followers of Cesar Millan. I don't mean 'fans'. Fans might just appreciate some of Mr. Millan's contributions to dog issues, such as getting people to walk more with their pets. I do.

All this leads to a problem. You see, the entertainment industry probably can afford lawyers. In fact, I'd venture to guess they have one or two lying around. Only a fool would denounce a beloved American TV show in writing.

So what do you do when you see a major problem you feel is harming animals, but speaking out may cost you everything? You do the right thing. You pussyfoot around the subject and hope to heaven you have a pair of clean panties left to your name when the dust settles.

Now where was I? Oh yes, as far as I could tell the volunteers' sole qualification in overriding the Three Springs' positive training protocol for dog handling was that they scrupulously studied Dog Whisperer shows.

To be fair, Bipsy and Pipsy may have even read Cesar's Way, but I bet their lips moved. A phenomenon is occurring, which the nation's trainers, behavioralists and animal keepers are witnessing at an alarming rate. *The Dog Whisperer show is harming animals! Tragically, after a few episodes, Millaners dub themselves expert dog trainers. Some of them may even own a dog. None of them can be deprogrammed.

In order to make some form of a point while perched delicately on eggshells, I'll summarize a few experiences I have had at various shelters, some as far away as Thailand. TV is everywhere. All hail Cesar!

That young couple? They were waiting for the dogs to wait and let them pass through the gate first. Why? Apparently this was to show who was in charge. Funny thing is, I thought I was in charge.

Funnier still, between volunteers and staff, the two confused rottweilers are walked by a dozen different people each month. Heaven help Dagwood if he has to guess the training approach (or lack there of) used by each of them.

Eventually Veronica and Dagwood surrendered. They were just turning back to see if their favorite soap was on television when the couple inexplicably walked out the gate. The dogs were yet again thrilled to be on their way. As the keeper in charge, this was the scary part for me.

Once I realize Millaners have infiltrated our ranks I have to stay vigilant. Would they get deep into the pine trees, then have an issue with one of the dogs? Instead of blowing the volunteer whistle, they might channel their inner TV trained trainerness, and try to imitate a bite with their finger tips or shove Veronica to the ground. Pardon my French, but with the type of dogs that I work with, that shit don't fly!

Outdated training techniques, especially full contact approaches, must not be launched at shelter dogs from left field. When inflicted by a stranger, it's just asking for the dog to make a mistake, misread the situation and bite. When television-viewing zealots decide they know best and ultimately inflict a bite history on a dog, it is a choice which can curse the dog's file and the dog's life forever.

According to his file, one of the most loyal and huggable dogs I have ever worked with was said to be a former Cesar Millan dog. Whether that was on TV, at Cesar's Dog Psychology Center or in some TV-Trainer's home, I cannot confirm. The results I can confirm.

A volunteer heard that Red was a "Cesar Dog." Red came to the shelter after he bit his owner. Surprise! Surprise! The owner was trying a Dog Whisperer Technique when it happened. Time passed. There were no further problems. Then Red bit again. Why?

The volunteer working with Red admitted (after the fact, and prior to the stitches), that he had grabbed

80 pound Red by the scruff and tried to pull him to the ground. He was a proud Millaner and had heard Red was a Cesar dog.

As a result, Red can no longer be worked with by volunteers and gets much less individual attention. Furthermore, he has fewer chances to show people what a spectacular animal he is. Potential adoptive homes are very limited.

Indeed, because two people receive cable television, this magnificent animal will likely spend his last few years on Earth at the shelter, waiting for an adoptive family that will never come for him.

I once had another Millaner Zealot couple (they tend to pair bond), tell me they were putting down their second English bulldog in three years due to aggression issues. Just last month it bit the husband, Tony. All Tony had done was try to push the dog to the ground when it was fighting with another dog in the park. "We're avid fans of The Dog Whisperer," they mentioned repeatedly.

"Really? I never would have guessed," I mumbled (speaking Latin for no f---ing shit).

Mrs. Tony cried as she relayed the tale of the bite incident. Catch a visual on this scene. Chippy, the bulldog, with a known history of dog aggression, is walking with his owners. He is, of course, unmuzzled in a public park. Yet, Tony and his little miss let him pass close to another dog. Surprise! Surprise! A dog fight breaks out!

So, what is the next obvious step? Tony, a retired white collar worker, reaches into a dog fight and attempts to push his dog to the ground. Chippy, frothing with rage and still fighting another dog is supposed to stop defending himself and swan dive into a calm submissive state of mind. Gosh, I can't imagine why the poor dog could ever have mistakenly bit his owner. Can you?

Now call me a silly goose, but I'm thinking maybe this is why there is a disclaimer at the start of The Dog Whisperer. I'm also thinkin' this is maybe precisely what Cesar Millan does not want untrained people to do. That is just my guess. But, no dog lover could.

That's where we have a problem. Most people are too full of themselves to admit they are clueless. I get that. But, I have never met people so sure they were right or so determined that organizations' rules and instructions don't apply to them as Millaners. They turn up everywhere determined to show animal care professionals the error of our ways. And, they listen to nothing. You'd think they had little David Koresh dolls wedged inside their ear canals.

Who would advocate pushing a pet to the ground so another dog could continue attacking it? No one. The 'Tonys' quick leap onto the euthanasia table was also very un-pro-training. Doesn't the Dog Whisperer TV program usually show pets with behavioral problems being worked with and not killed?

I'm not surprised Tony and the little miss missed the point. I offered advice, called a trainer in to talk to them and suggested possible placement options in the event they did not wish to keep their bulldog. Nothing deterred them. It was obvious they felt they had properly followed Cesar's way and the dog was just defective, their second defective dog. How very odd.

Like his predecessor, Chippy was euthanized two days later. But it's okay, the duo already had a third English bulldog puppy on order. I personally would have recommended a different breed for them, perhaps one made by Lego®. I would also have recommended a period of mourning. During this time they could pull their heads out of their asses.

Another place I worked at actually had to have security escort a job applicant off the property four days into his trial week. Once management told him to cease practicing Dog Whisperer (or his version of) techniques on the animals, did he stop? Oh, hell no! He just snuck dogs out when no one was looking and continued his maniacal behavior without hesitation.

Did he get the job? Oh, hell no! The only real question is who would let this dumb ass make it to a trial week in the first place? How hard is it to ask, "What training technique do you follow?" during the interview?

Before you send your letters, realize I'm not bashing Cesar Millan. Heck, if anyone as hot looking as Will Smith will vouch for the man, that is good enough for me. I am, however, bashing the Dog Whisperer television show's Zealot Millan Worshipers. Clear enough?

Remember, with proper editing and the right background music, Hollywood can make picking your nose into an attractive and adventurous new trend. That doesn't mean we should all walk through the dog park doing it.

I can't help but wonder, if little ol' me has been confronted by so many problems resulting from this television show in under six months (that's right), what happens if you add up all the tens of thousands of other dog handlers and trainers around the world? It's no secret that this issue keeps popping up everywhere. Cumulatively, how many dogs have been harmed?

Now, to my understanding, it's less than practical to have a TV show without an audience. This show needs to go! Its viewers cause too much damage!*

*It would seem counterintuitive to put a disclaimer at the end of an article that resulted from people who (in my opinion) ignore a television show's disclaimer. Nonetheless . . . That's my personal opinion. Other opinions may vary. Must be 21 to enter. Not valid in states of ND, CT, denial or confusion. Letters of complaint may be sent to: Millaners@DontBeAWanker.com

The Labrador Retriever is not only the most popular pet dog breed in the United States, but also in Canada and the United Kingdom.

Nola Lee Kelsey

Kids vs. Dogs

Irresponsibly letting dogs reproduce results in suffering and an overburdened animal sheltering system. Irresponsibly reproducing ourselves causes human suffering and is overburdening our planet to the point that very soon now, it will kill us all.

"Wait a moment, Nola," you may be thinking. "This book is supposed to be funny. You can't tell us to save ourselves by not dropping babies like rabbits loose in a Viagra factory. That's not funny."

I apologize! You are right. Global decimation is not funny. I only meant to compare dogs and kids, but I got carried away.

Having spent decades both raising children and rescuing animals, I speak from experience. So, to heck with environmental Tipping Points and good ol' eradication of life. There are more important reasons why adopting a dog is better than having children. I don't need logic on my side just to prove a point. Dogs are just better. Think about it.

When you bring home a puppy, you need to budget for a fence and a bag of dog food. When you bring home a child, you're in it for three cars, a college education, and some funky fruit thing called a Blackberry®.

Dogs are a ten to eighteen year commitment. Kids linger a minimum of twenty-two years. Not to mention, dogs never move back in when they are forty, bringing along their second husband and a litter.

And can anyone explain to me why children need to be driven to soccer practice three times a week? Yet dogs have a perfectly good time just playing with a soccer ball in the backyard.

I personally paid for 15 years of martial arts classes for my son Jerry. Yet my untrained 17 lb terrier can take down three bikers and a nun without breaking a sweat.

Kids make things so complicated. If a dog wants a steak to eat, he just finds one thawing on the kitchen counter and helps himself. Kids expect you to cook their meat, serve it, and, get this: I've been told parents are supposed to clean up afterwards.

At 14, teenagers hate everything about their parents. A two year old golden retriever (14 in people years) could not be a more loyal companion.

On some level society must understand it's more important to keep pets safe than kids. When I walk my dog on a leash I am considered a good and responsible person. When I walk kids on a leash it's not nearly as acceptable. It may be the muzzle that disturbs people most.

And have you ever noticed that when your dog steals your beer and spills half of it on the floor, he immediately licks up the mess instead of pulling a throw rug over the stain and claiming the house was robbed?

I, for one, have never come back from the movies to discover my Dalmatian has thrown a kegger and there are three poodles and a mastiff passed out on his bed. Plus, I rarely find porn stashed under the dog bed.

Who cares if your kid is potty trained by fourteen months? My puppy quit pissing on the floor at eight weeks. And, FYI: he could walk by then, too.

Most important of all, puppies can be spayed or neutered by the time they are two pounds or six months of age. Child Protective Services has recently informed me that this is "a big no, no" when human children are involved, even if one million more are being born every four days.

Did you know dogs are actually not color blind? According to Scientists, dogs see a different quality of color. It's similar to a person viewing colors at twilight.

Nola Lee Kelsey

Sex and the Single Dog Fighter

Few things in life are less sexy than men who drive Humvees®. They scream over-inflated ego inside. Why not just hang a sign on yourself that says, "Hey there everyone, I'm so cool I don't need to leave a healthy planet to my children. Besides I think I need bulletproof windows in my car. P.S. I'm over-compensating for having an intensely miniscule pecker." Yes, that is a big sign.

Whoopee! Slice me off a hunk of that man.

So, what could be a bigger turnoff than superficial, eco-scourge? Dogfighters, of course! Obviously, we have plummeted far beyond the Small Pecker Zone when these scum-suckers turn up. Although in the United States a person has the right to be "Pecker Free and Proud to Be," violence against innocents is unacceptable!

Seventy percent of dogfighters or other animal abuse offenders have also been arrested for violent crimes against people. Often those who abuse people start out abusing animals, then escalate. Given these statistics, what could be even more irksome than dogfighters?

Who else could vex me so? Airport security? Manufacturers of liquid cheese? Nope! The winner is; women who love dogfighters. I mean seriously gals, what the guacamole could you be thinking?

Wow! Here comes that sexy Lil' Willie from down the block. Oh look, he stole more cute puppies to use in his fighting dog's bait bag. Maybe once he's done burying the bodies, he'll wash off the blood and we can procreate. Hot diggitty!

I've always wanted to 'do' a violence-prone man. He even hides out in a basement full of other losers while forcing animals to tear the flesh from one other. That's peachy great news! He'll make fine daddy for my nine kids, because I know he'll never hit us after a long hard day of animal abuse. Heck I'm getting hot just thinking about that Lil' Willie. Oh baby. Oh baby.

Hey, if you get really lucky, maybe he'll even reek of generic cigarettes and cheap beer. Score! At least when Lil' Willie leaves you for your thirteen year old daughter, you can try to do better.

Of course, if you're happy at this level of society, might I recommend trying a foursome with Mike Vick and those two puppy-tossing Marines? Surely one of them will pan out to meet your low social standards, no doubt whisking you away to a wonderful life. Though I suspect Mr. Vick's 'dance card' is full until Cell Block C is finished with him, a girl can always dream.

Seriously ladies, you have the power to change the world! Use it. If each of you cuts off sex for men who dog fight and/or drive Hummers, you'd be making a major contribution to the Earth and its future generations.

Heaven knows we don't need a single dogfighter's genetic material lapping our gene pool. And I'm willing to bet the egos of most Humvee drivers need a beautiful woman hanging off their arms more than they need the ability to shop for shoes on the streets of Sadr City.

So, let's all get out there and do our part to save the planet, shall we? Leave your favorite dogfighter alone to play with his cattle prod. Proudly walk past any man in a vehicle that gets less than 35 MPG. Seek out those gentle, unsuspecting, earth-friendly gentlemen driving hybrids and Geos. Then, ravish them for days. If they ride a moped, ravish them twice.

It's all in the name of making the world a better place. And, if you happen to get pregnant along the way, who would you honestly want raising your child?

Think you need a purebred? According to The
Humane Society of the United States,
around 24% of animals in shelters are purebreds.
There are also many breed specific rescues full of dogs
needing good homes.

Nola Lee Kelsey

Five Things to Know

Let's cut to the chase, shall we? Here are five things I wish non-dog people would keep in mind.

1) If you do not have a dog, it is likely you are not a "dog person." You may like dogs. You may have treasured childhood memories of a dog. You may someday evolve into being a dog-person. But the phrase "dog person" is reserved to describe those of us for whom it is biologically impossible to function more than 12 consecutive weeks without a second heart beating at knee level. There is no insult intended when

I say you aren't a dog person. It's just reality. Deal with it!

2) My dogs are my children; hence, they live in my home. When I go to your house and trip all over your recalled Chinese toys, I always manage to smile politely. I do this despite watching drippy snot run down your kid's three chins. When you are in my house you will be adorned with dog hair on your clothes and are expected to smile politely whenever drool enters the scene.

3) At 5:00 in the morning, when the entire 5 acre park is empty, there is absolutely no excuse for a lone jogger to veer off the sidewalk and run straight by a woman walking three dogs far off in the grass. If you don't see the problem here, visit WhyDidIJustGetBit.com.

4) When I am breaking up a dog fight, please do not demand my attention by walking up recommending a book you just read, listing what you need from the grocery store or commenting on the chimes of the new doorbell. Are you kidding? I may

project calmness, but you are throwing gasoline on an open flame. Calm or not, until the animals are put away and I stop the bleeding, it's not about you!

5) And finally, claiming you "love dogs" is not the way to get a date with me. Thanks to my ex, I can spot, and distinguish between, bull-shit, horse shit and dog shit from a distance of over five miles.

For the record, when I ask dog-less men sniffing around my front door (the once every 5 years it happens) to walk my dogs with me, it is a test. So far, all have failed. We don't even need to meander more than three feet for me to evaluate your potential as a date or mate.

You see, it does not matter if you get irritated when Koko drags you through the park like you're an Iditarod sled. It won't even matter if you are too genetically humorless to notice that my darling Henry looks like a space alien. Never mind if you are so totally oblivious to animals that you don't see Flipper slip off his harness and head into the forest to hunt big game. Most men don't make it that far.

If your eyes do not sparkle when my pack walks out the front door, if the sight of such comedy does not launch you into fits of laughter and awe, if you do not gleefully swan dive into the whole squirming pile of teeth and hair, and if you do not ask to know all of their histories immediately (as I would of your dogs), we have no potential to go on a date. We'd both be bored to tears. Been there, done that.

5.5) By the way, if you are thinking of trying to make an impression by tying my two loves together and telling me how you unknowingly ate dog meat in Thailand, don't. I hear it weekly. Conjuring up one more fake smile and an aren't-you-so-worldly nod will kill me. Please! Just impale my skull with a Rupert Holmes album and be done with it.

Enough said!

In 2002 a book written by Thailand's King Bhumibol Adulyadej about his pet dog (who was born a stray) sold 100,000 copies in less than half a day.

Nola Lee Kelsey

The Gift that Keeps on Giving

At this point, I must take a moment and ask members of my family to skip past this chapter. Thank you!

I didn't want to ruin their surprise. I've stumbled on all their future Birthday and Christmas presents. As for the rest of you, put down the car keys. Burn those well-worn mall walking shoes. There will be no more wondering, "What will I get my wife for our anniversary – last week." Never again will you ponder how to find the right present for cousin Mindy's Baby Shower or Puppy Adoption. I've discovered the ultimate in multi-faceted, form-fitting, gender-crossing, heavily-hyphenated, species-neutral gifts.

Last week while I was planted head first in our rescue's toy donation bin, I came upon this miracle of modern science. At first I thought my eyes were deceiving me, so I grabbed the stuffed toy and swam for the surface. Even in the light of the staff room, I had doubts.

The toy was plush, double-dachshund long, and had a curly textured surface. Could it be? Fortunately the tag was still attached. It confirmed my wildest hopes. I had discovered The Original Loofa Dog®! What a combination! Only the most fabulous of minds could have done such a thing.

The tag went on to read, "This funky dog toy can be used as a retriever and a back scratcher." That's right folks, now after a hard afternoon of playing fetch with Binky, you can fling this handy toy over your own back. Clutch both ends, and give yourself a back scratching to remember. But wait! There's more!

Let us not forget it's a loofa. Once Skeeter has had his fun you can take Loofa Dog into the shower and exfoliate yourself into a coma. Civilization has hit its pinnacle.

First fire, then the wheel, now Loofa Dog! But wait! There's still more! Naturally I went home that night and made a beeline for the Loofa Dog website. As it turns out, Loofa Dog is available in a multitude of designer colors for your fetching and facial pleasures. There is even a pink Loofa Dog to increase pet play, decrease blackheads and promote breast cancer awareness. Viva la versatility! What more could we hope for?

Lest you think I am the only one who has recognized the glory of this multitasking toy, Loofa Dog is actually the "Award Winning Loofa Dog." That's right! You heard it here last. According to the Multipet International website, I had stumbled upon the recipient of "Pet Business Magazine's 2007 Pet Industry Recognition Award for Outstanding Dog Toy." Eureka! Was there ever any doubt?

But, hold onto your bladder. Multipet now sells a "Mini Loofa Dog®" for all your small dog needs and, I imagine, for cleaning those pesky hard to reach spots behind your ears.

But wait! There is still, still more! For not only can you purchase the original and Mini Loofa Dog, you can also add Bungee Loofa Dog® to your collection. Why stop at exercising Spot and exercising good personal hygiene, when you can also use your Loofa Dog for strapping your Harley into the truck bed (in a variety of designer colors).

And hey, did I mention that Loofa Dog squeaks? Yes, with just a gentle squeeze of your loofa the bathroom turns into a symphony of tantalizing tunes for your listening pleasure - until the moment Duke body-slams himself through the shower door to retrieve his favorite toy.

Is this not the gift that keeps on giving? But wait! Not only is this dog playing, ear reaching, super exfoliating, Harley Davidson® strapping product available in a mixed brew of colors and sizes, there are also seasonally appropriate Loofa Dogs for the holidays! You guessed it, those fab folks at Multipet sell a Halloween Loofa Dog®, dressed in a little witch's hat, which I can only guess would also serve as a dental pick for both you and your pet. There's still,

still, still more! Christmas Loofa Dog® is a stocking stuffer, too!

I, for one, am waiting for a Thanksgiving Loofa Dog which could be used as a festive centerpiece at family dinners, then later be used to remove dry skin from the feet of house guests who linger too long in tryptophan stupors.

Now there is a point at which one can only handle so much in-depth internet shopping without appropriate bladder control protection, but it was difficult not to look on with sense of awe and frivolity at some of the other Multipet products. Take for example, the Shammy Lammy® and Seaweeds Friends® toys. Yes, it is true. You can now purchase a complete collection of kelp-themed dog toys for those occasions when nothing but a plush marine invertebrate will satisfy your bloodhound's needs. I won't even start on the "Wiggly Giggly®," available for canines and equines.

As my eyes grew weary, I spotted another stuffed toy. This one resembled Gonzo from the Muppets and was called Flea®. Foolishly, I read the product details. "Now your dog can bite back! Our line of cuddly fleas are the perfect revenge for canine companions…" Oh please let there be room on my credit card!

Now, I am in no way promoting illegal drug use here, but if you happen to live in California® and are being treated for glaucoma®, might I recommend that you whittle away your post-prescription hours by surfing the Multipet website?

As you can well imagine, Flea pushed me over the edge. I fell straight out of my wiggly giggly office chair®. Luckily the impact was lessened when I landed on my new stash of Emergency Airbag Loofa Dogs®, in a variety of designer colors for all my holiday needs.

Mankind could learn many things from dogs: to be a true friend, to be faithful, to appreciate those who love him, and to always share his loofa.

Nola Lee Kelsey

The Fish Whisperer

As I meander towards the end stages of another book and prepare to inflict my numerous grammatical offences on my editors, Jeanne and Valerie, a certain irony is forming outside the dog-hair-enveloped bubble that is my life. Alas, I foresee the end of dog books being popular. In fact, I sense that the end of dogs and cats being kept as pets at all may be looming near. A new player has entered the field.

A curious new pet trend is emerging and there is something fishy about the entire scenario. As I randomly scramble commas (or comas) with hyphens, big news is breaking. Comet the Wonder Fish is taking the world by storm! And, what a world it is.

As of last week, Comet was poised to seize the record of most goldfish tricks learned by outperforming Albert Einstein, a calico fantail. Millions are glued to their televisions. Some are even paying attention to what's on them.

Meanwhile, Comet shocked the sports world by shooting hoops like Mike Jordan (thanks to extreme float time), bending it like Beckham (someday someone can tell me what the hell that means), and navigating the agility slalom better than Bandito the Border collie.

How could a fish conquer the sports world you ask? The planet's new-found fish trainer extraordinaire, Dr. Dean Pomerleau, used positive reinforcement training techniques, teaching Comet to perform his vast repertoire of the fish tricks (not to be mistaken for fish sticks).

Thanks to his handy R2 Fish School Training Kit, not only is Dr. Pomerleau's wonder fish drifting towards the pinnacle of athleticism, but Comet rounded out his international YouTube debut by outlimboing every other fish in his tank. Only moments after the cameras shut off, Comet signed a contract to appear on next season's Dancing with the Stars. Dr. Phil producers are also fishing around.

As goldfish mania bubbles over, National Geographic Channel is seizing the opportunity. A three season deal has just been struck with that charismatic Metrosexual and famed assistant fish groomer, Cedar Mellon. He will be teaching all Earth a "better" way to handle their scaly, but loveable pets.

Mellon stepped forward promptly and informed the world that there are better ways than positive reinforcement training (and, don't we all hate that 'positive' shit?). Based on his vast experience of eating fish many times when he was a child in Peru, Mellon has devised the following guidelines for his new approach to pet fish handling.

1) Never let your fish leave the tank ahead of you or he will become a dominating and unruly bastard.

2) If your fish gets wound up and becomes aggressive, push him down and hold him on the

sidewalk until he enters a calm submissive state of mind.

3) When your fish fails to obey smack it on the side of the neck with a suction cup. This imitates the way mother dog fish discipline unruly pup fish.

4) Your fish should always walk beside or behind you. Never let him lead you, your pack, school or pod. If you do, he'll take over your life and any small businesses you own. (Note: We just don't ask why this unholy domination does not occur when your pet pulls you, thus leading you, on roller blades through Central Park's paddle boating pond.)

5) And finally, remember to always project a calm and confident assertiveness. Aquarium fish, especially sea horses, can smell fear.

Cedar is adamant that he has never encountered a fish he could not help. In fact, if during the show he encounters an owner who can't be trained to handle his fish properly, Cedar will bring the animal in for extra help at his New York City based Fish Psychology Center (FPC), located in a large drainage ditch behind Sacs Fifth Avenue.

The Center is filled with once cantankerous koi, perch, guppies and hag fish all living symbiotically under a rainbow together. Kumbaya!

Better still the FPC is using Nat Geo's popularity to launch a new merchandise line. Their first product is, The Delusion Collar. "This will be a great training aid for aquarium owners who need extra assistance handling their problematic fish," says FPC sales representative, Shirley Ugest.

The Delusion Collar itself bares a striking resemblance to the fish jar necklace worn by Bill Murray in 'What About Bob.' However, according to Ms. Ugest, the 'collar' is worn backwards so the fish does not establish himself as pack leader. She adds, when used properly (which only Cedar can), Mr. Mellon feels any jackass off the street can rehabilitate even the most aggressive Beta (fighting fish), allowing them to school in harmony with other fish.

Meanwhile zealot fans of the soon to be un-trendy Dog Whisperer Show are dumping mere mammalian pets at animal shelters in alarming numbers. Then they are flooding electronic stores buying up extra batteries for their remote controls.

Former Millan groupie (not to be confused for a grouper), Ima Wannabe says, "I've always wanted a pet guppy named Alfonso, but thought it might be too much for me to handle. Now that I have watched one pilot episode of The Fish Whisperer, I think I am the hottest fucking animal trainer since Siegfried and Roy went on hiatus."

As you can imagine, the world's top fish trainers are concerned. "It saddens me to see Cedar Mellon's Fish Whisperer fans trying these methods at home in their own tanks," say handler Inoha Whatimdoin. "He's set animal training back thirty years." Later that same day, the author of the renowned fish training manual, *The Other End of the Air Hose*, added, "Mellon is a fruit. His techniques may play well when edited for TV, but a few weeks later many of these fish are winding up in shelters or being euthanized, and stir fried, outright. Several have even attacked small children." But, Fish Whisperer fans do not heed the warnings. Surprise!

The delusion is getting worse. Thousands of armchair Fish Whispering zealots are now under the belief that they are marine biologists. They've been spotted swarming to the world's coral reefs and behaving condescendingly to professional Marine Science Researchers. Mellon fans insist they must establish themselves as Alphas over swarms of belligerent nudibranchs and nervous sea cucumbers.

Comet the Wonder Fish, who is two (that is 150 in dog years), issued his own press release about the controversy.

"Just how stupid are people?"

Well said, Comet. As a writer I have met my equal in this fabulously finned friend to all. I hold no grudges that a goldfish is undermining my business of dog writing. In fact, as a former marine park keeper, I have plenty of tales to tell. I may just flop onto this bandwagon myself.

While my Editors tend to doubt that *Fish: Funny Side Up!* would work well for a book title, I see potential. Of course, I'm currently wearing a Delusion Collar.

Admittedly, the image of fish surrounded by barbeque equipment on my cover might not offer quite the humorous effect I was shooting for. Still, if Comet can be trained to cook a dogfighter, I'm willing to give it a shot. "Paging Dr. Pomerleau."

Contrary to the pessimist's view, dogs are actually loyal to their owners out of companionship and caring not because we give them food.

Nola Lee Kelsey

C.R.A.P. Index

In recognition of the fact that my opinions may not meet the Politically Correct trends of today's uptight society, I have provided the following Currently Recognized As Pissed (C.R.A.P.) Index. Listed below are people, organizations, communities and the like whom I am already fully aware I have aggravated. If you are mad at me for stating my personal views please refer to this handy reference. If your name appears as C.R.A.P., there is no reason to bother writing me.

If you are not C.R.A.P. and feel you deserve to be, please register complaints through our website at:

www.DontBeAWanker.com. All necessary applications to be considered C.R.A.P. will be returned back to you along with boat-loads of spam.

- Puppy Mills
- Advocates of BS Legislation
- Denver City Council
- Ohio
- Pet Stores
- The Maker of Excalibur®
- Puppy Tossing Marines
- The Marine Corp
- Private Evil Grinninfuck
- Private Evil Grinninfuck's Incestuous Grampy
- Michael Vick
- Cell Block 'C'
- Designer Dog Breeders
- All Dog Breeders
- PETA (*Psychotics for the Endangerment of True Activism?)

- Fireworks Manufacturers
- Snow Men
- Gnomes
- Airline Security
- Bad Pet Sitters
- Shrew
- Jolly Rodger
- Candi the Klepto Cashier®
- Ernest
- Animal Hoarders
- Millaners
- Melloners
- The Tonys
- Advertisers Whose Money Supports the Dog Whisperer Show
- Producers of Dog Whisperer
- Parents
- Humvee Drivers
- Humvee Manufacturers
- Dogfighters

- White Trash
- Men
- Cedar Mellon
- Belligerent Nudibranchs®

*Other opinions may vary!

Thank you and have a nice day!

"God...sat down for a moment when the dog was finished in order to watch it...and to know that it was good, that nothing was lacking, that it could not have been made better."

Rainer Maria Rilke

Care for Dogs

Lek in Buddha's arms,
Wat Chedi Luang,
Chiangmai, Thailand

Learn more about Thailand's temple and street (soi)
dogs by visiting the Care for Dogs website at:

www.CareForDogs.org

Other domestic animal rescues across Thailand include:

Noistar Thai Animal Rescue Foundation (Koh Tao):
http://www.kohtaoanimalclinic.org

Soi Cat and Dog Bangkok: http://www.scadbangkok.org

Dog Rescue Center Samui: http://www.samuidog.org

Lanna Dog Rescue (Chiangmai): http://www.lannadog.net

Head Rock Dogs (Hau Hin): http://www.headrockdogs.org

Soi Dog Foundation (Pucket): http://www.soidog.org

PhaNgan Animal Care (Koh PhaNgan):
http://pacthailand.org On August 1, 2008, just as their
upgraded facility neared completion, PAC was destroyed by
an arson fire. Follow their story and learn how you can help
the only rescue on this island by visiting PAC's website.

More Dog's Eye View Media Books
by Nola Lee Kelsey

Let's Go Visit Best Friends Animal Sanctuary
Infused with laughter and colorful photographs, *Let's Go Visit Best Friends Animal Sanctuary* is designed to be read aloud in home, library, or classroom settings and to encourage conversation with children about kindness to animals and responsible pet ownership. Edited by award winning children's author Jeanne Modesitt. Photographed by Nola Lee Kelsey and Alan K. Anderson (www.reflectedsun.com). ISBN: 978-0-9802323-0-1

Bitch Unleashed : The Harsh Realities of Goin' Country
(Revised for 2008) A wicked, gut-wrenching, satire for despondent urban refugees, flabbergasted backyard farmers and devotees of evil mirth. Edited by Valerie Stone of SIQ Consulting & Research. ISBN: 978-0-9802323-1-8

The Night Before a Dogtown Christmas
A whimsical take on a holiday classic, written by former Dogtown Caregiver, Nola Lee Kelsey. Illustrated by renowned contemporary artist Avonelle Kelsey, this unique title brings real, thinking art to the world of children's books. (www.AvonelleKelsey.com) ISBN: 978-0-9802323-4-9

Order by title, author and/or ISBN # through your local independent booksellers or national chain stores. From your favorite online shop search for books by Nola Lee Kelsey.

★ Dogs: Funny Side Up! Merchandise
Buy your always stylish "Dogfighters Have Tiny Peckers" tote bag, or a wildly coveted "Save a Pit Bull - Barbecue a Dogfighter" BBQ apron, along with other gloriously abrasive merchandise! Visit the Dogs: Funny Side Up store at: www.CafePress.com/NolaKelsey

A Note to My Readers

Dear Readers,

I need your help! For several years now I have produced books which resulted in an overwhelming amount of positive feedback from my readers. Apparently many of you love my stuff. In fact, in California, Librarians may soon be allowed to legally marry several of my titles.

True, my quirky, off-beat, occasionally abrasive satire is not for everyone. For the time being it's apparently not for the "big publishing houses". Perhaps I am just too hypersensitive or too lazy to spend a year writing a book proposal, then wait months for a generic letter of rejection. I, of course, prefer to think of myself as relentlessly determined. I won't stop writing books I enjoy.

As a result, in late 2007, I started my own publishing company, Dog's Eye View Media (DEVM). DEVM is devoted to bringing you titles from a mixed-brew of authors, each offering you some laughter and education with books that look at the world from a different angle.

Like any new independent business, word of mouth advertising is the life blood of my company. That means you are my life blood. If you enjoy a DEVM book, please take the time to recommend it to others, write and post reviews, talk the book up on social networking sites, give copies as gifts, donate them to libraries, hire skywriters, etc.

As I write this letter to my readers, I have five different books pouring out of me. I couldn't stop them if I tried. Nonetheless, without rallying the support of my fan-base, my ability to bring these titles to market may soon come to an end. So, if you enjoy my work, please help spread the word! Someday your funny-bone will thank you for it.

Thank you,

Nola Lee Kelsey

Yes!

Printed in the United States
126397LV00001B/28-75/P